# Bonsai Design:
# Deciduous and Coniferous trees

## Peter D. Adams

WARD LOCK

First published in Great Britain in 1990
by Ward Lock Limited, Villiers House,
41/47 Strand, London WC2N 5JE, England.

A Cassell Imprint

House editor Denis Ingram
Designed by Gwyn Lewis

Text filmset in Great Britain
by August Filmsetting, Haydock, St Helens
Printed and bound in Italy
by OFSA spa

British Library Cataloguing in Publication Data
Adams, Peter D. (Peter David), *1939 —*
    Bonsai design.
    1. Bonsai. Cultivation
    I. Title
    635.9772

ISBN 0 7063 6836 3

# Contents

## PART ONE. THE PROFILES

# PART TWO. THE CASE HISTORIES

*This book is dedicated to my family.*

# Author's Acknowledgements

I am indebted to Dan Barton, Rob Hadley, Jonathan Harrison and Dave Sampson for the majority of the photographs. Other photographic material and all line drawings are by the author.

# Publisher's Note

Readers are requested to note that references to months and seasons in the text are appropriate to the northern hemisphere. It is hoped that readers in the southern hemisphere will find the following conversion chart helpful:

| NORTHERN HEMISPHERE | | | | SOUTHERN HEMISPHERE |
|---|---|---|---|---|
| Mid-winter | = | January | = | Mid-summer |
| Late winter | = | February | = | Late summer |
| Early spring | = | March | = | Early autumn |
| Mid-spring | = | April | = | Mid-autumn |
| Late spring | = | May | = | Late autumn |
| Early summer | = | June | = | Early winter |
| Mid-summer | = | July | = | Mid-winter |
| Late summer | = | August | = | Late winter |
| Early autumn | = | September | = | Early spring |
| Mid-autumn | = | October | = | Mid-spring |
| Late autumn | = | November | = | Late spring |
| Early winter | = | December | = | Early summer |

# Preface

To be successful, Bonsai depend upon both sound horticulture and aesthetics for their visual impact. This book attempts to demonstrate in terms of the best production techniques for deciduous and coniferous species, how the splice of horticulture and aesthetics produces Bonsai.

The book carries a profile of the species mentioned which will contain everything you need to know about habitat, specific horticulture, training techniques and a monthly programme of suggested steps covering the initial six or seven year period.

Part Two looks at actual older Bonsai of the mentioned species, discussing the steps involved in the evolution of the individual tree. This section is really a case history of programmes that have worked and are offered as training aids rather than masterpieces, in the hope that they may stimulate an idea or a chain of images that may help with this thorny problem of design that I am constantly asked about by my students.

For the most part in each profile, I have described the development of a simple 'informal' tree with a curving trunk to act as a basic learning vehicle as I fed in the differences dictated by the horticultural needs of each species.

P.D.A.

# PART ONE. THE PROFILES

# 1 Profile on Beech and Hornbeam

## Natural habitat and plant description

*Fagus*, or Beech, is found distributed from America across Europe to Asia. It is a magnificent tree, often reaching 30 m (100 ft) or more and the form is broadly broom shaped.

Old trees display a silvered bark that is a metallic-like grey and most appealing. The young leaves are fresh lettuce green and soft and are up to 10 cm (4 in) in length. The winter buds are sharply pointed and clothed with light brown leaves that cling on as a natural frost protection. Where cold nights and late season sunny daytime weather combine to help trap the sugars in the foliage, the autumn colour is a magnificent display of yellows, burnt orange and russet. The leaf of *Fagus sylvatica*, the common Beech, has around six pairs of veins and has a gently rippled edge. The salad green matures to a deeper, more glossy green. The growth pattern of the shoots is slightly kinked towards each leaf and this alternating form gives a zigzag impression.

There are many ancient Beech hedgerows in the UK and often old tall trees will produce natural layers as their lowest branches dip down and are covered with leaf mould. There are excellent dwarfed Beeches in the mountains of the UK and throughout Europe.

*F. crenata*, the Japanese Beech, is similar to *F. sylvatica* but differs in its smaller leaves and in its white bark which is as bright as Silver Birch. In general terms, *F. crenata* is a weaker tree in Bonsai culture than the common Beech.

*Carpinus*, or Hornbeam, has the same geographical range as the Beech. It is a beautiful tree very similar to the Beech in size and general appearance and differs mainly in the brown striping on the grey bark and in the deep fluting around the bole.

The form is broadly broom shaped and branches tend to meander in sinuous fashion, with the twigs inclining slightly to zigzag like the Beech. The general shape and colour of the leaf is similar

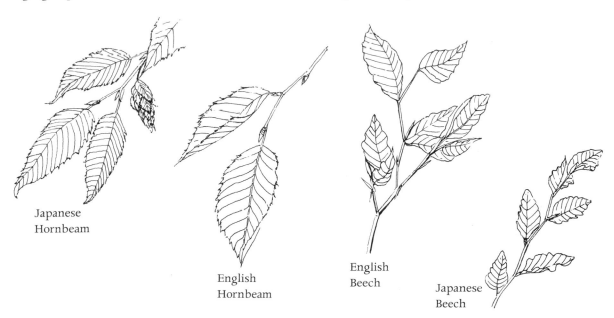

Japanese
Hornbeam

English
Hornbeam

English
Beech

Japanese
Beech

15

Japanese Beech

to the Beech and most people confuse them at first. The obvious differences are the Hornbeam's greater number of veins – about 15, in the case of *Carpinus betulus*, the European Hornbeam – the sharper ribbing of the vein and saw edges of the leaf.

Catkins are freely produced in spring and are followed by hop-like fruits which make a pretty display in summer. In general, the foliage darkens to deep green and then to yellow gold in autumn. The leaves are retained through the winter.

There are forms of Hornbeam which produce bright red young growth, including *C. turczaninowii*, a Hornbeam from China and Korea. *C. caroliniana*, the American Hornbeam, also displays autumn tints.

## Horticultural preferences as Bonsai

### Soil

Both Beech and Hornbeam do well in open soil. I use a lot of sand in the soil mix and favour a round type of sand particle if this is available. A range of sizes between 2–3 mm is ideal for the main soil with 4–6 mm ($\frac{1}{8}$–$\frac{1}{4}$ in) providing a good lower soil that breathes. The round sand produces a gentler type of branch growth typical of the elegant nature of these species. Round sand admits the invasion of root tips without cutting or dividing them and this is reflected in smoother top growth.

The second soil component is peat and long grained peat is superior in its water retentive properties.

The third component is leaf mould, well decomposed and sieved. Oak and Beech are best. The Beech favours its own litter and the Hornbeams often produce strands of mycelium in the soil mass. Such benevolent fungus among the roots is a sure sign of the tree's wellbeing and it should not be disturbed. In the wild, both Beech and Hornbeam produce layered lowered branches in the leaf mould that surrounds them.

The fourth component I now use, and one which works well for my students as well, is 'Arthur Bower's Ericaceous Compost'.

The final mixture is:

    4 parts sand
    2 parts peat
    2 parts leaf mould
    2 parts A.B.E.C.

16

Ensure that all ingredients are dry and then combine them and sieve away the fines. The soil should feel light in the hands. If it appears to look very dark try adding another part of sand. Although deciduous trees enjoy moisture, they also need to breathe and a good sand base to the mix will ensure the presence of air around the roots.

TABLE 1.1 *Water requirements of Beech and Hornbeam*

**Stage I** Plants in development. Generous watering encourages vigour.

| January | *Damp* |
|---|---|
| February | *Damp* |
| March | *Moist* |
| April | *Plenty of water* |
| May | *Plenty of water* |
| June | *Plenty of water* |
| July | *Plenty of water* |
| August | *Plenty of water* |
| September | *Plenty of water* |
| October | *Damp* |
| November | *Damp* |
| December | *Damp* |

**Stage II** Plants in structure and refinement.

| January | *Damp* |
|---|---|
| February | *Damp* |
| March | *Moist* |
| April | *Evenly damp* |
| May | *Evenly damp* |
| June | *Evenly damp* |
| July | *Evenly damp* |
| August | *Evenly damp* |
| September | *Evenly damp* |
| October | *Damp* |
| November | *Damp* |
| December | *Damp* |

Plants in development need copious water over leaves and soil. Plants in structure and refinement need almost as much but be careful not to encourage too much sappy growth. Keep foliage misted and cool.

# Water

Keep both Beech and Hornbeam species *evenly damp*. Young trees need a lot of water to spur shoot development, while mature plants will stay compact if a leaner regime is followed. Either way, avoid drought and deluge. Regular leaf spray is highly desirable. Trees in development need quick bulking out of leaves, twigs and trunk so that they thicken and produce plump, round wood that will respond to rigorous pruning with heavy bud production.

In years before the 'Greenhouse Effect', you could predict that water and feeding regimes, if accelerated during May and July, would produce massive shoot activity especially to Beech. In recent seasons, trees have been experiencing early stress due to incipient spring activity and therefore insufficient winter rest, followed by early hot spells. It is sensible under these conditions to provide a safety net of constant dampness to help smooth out the sudden peaks and to use shading to help conserve the moisture levels within the plants. Remember that these trees usually grow in light woodland, so the factors of shade, cool roots and constant moisture are all important.

# Transplanting
## Standard repotting
Follow usual Bonsai procedures, employing the recommended light soil. Up to one-third of the root mass may safely be removed. The best time to repot both species is just ahead of bud emergence. Watch for any splitting of the bud cases and then repot without delay.

## Repotting frequency
Young trees are repotted annually; trees up to ten years, every other year; older plants, every two or more seasons. The roots of Hornbeam are often very dense – almost like plywood in fact! It is important to clean out excessively crowded growth between all main roots. If root tips around the ends of the major surface roots are pruned only lightly, heavy buttressing may be encouraged as the extending lines strike out strongly, taking the trunk line with them. In all cases, be cautious about further soil watering after the initial watering in. The roots need oxygen too.

## Collecting procedures
Use a deep wooden box with plentiful drainage holes for establishing collected material. Ensure that there is a good drainage course. Follow the usual procedure of unwrapping the roots and then

transferring the root mass on to a layer of very open mix. I usually add 50% sand to the recommended soil mixture for this bottom layer. Below the trunk base, place an old tile, tin plate or the like, to prevent new roots going straight down. This also reinforces surface flare.

Arrange the roots as far as possible with the fingers. Clean up any damaged roots with a sharp knife. Often a web of shallow roots will have been produced and collection is therefore easy. In the violent storms recently experienced, uprooted Beeches have sometimes revealed a root depth of no greater than 15–30 cm (6–12 in)!

*Lay* further soil in and do not use pressure on the soil. Stabilize the tree by using guy ropes to tie the trunk to the box wall and remember to cushion the friction points on the trunk.

Place the box on blocks to provide air circulation below. Trees may be lost if the roots drown. Use Vitamin $B_1$ transplant solution and drench the soil. Mist the top regularly and *watch for the need to water the soil again.*

For many years I have successfully used poly tunnels to re-establish these species, as they like light humidity. I always ventilate the greenhouse well.

Be careful to shade all newly collected material. The embryonic and damaged root system will not be capable of supporting a soft spread of leaf if high temperatures are experienced. If the tree is not protected under these conditions, moisture is lost faster than the root system can supply it, and the plant dries up. Think of it as a cutting, and shade and mist the top for the first season.

## Containers

A simple seed box or wooden crate with good drainage is fine for recently collected or developing material. Remember to elevate the container on blocks for ventilation.

Plants which are being structured require an approximation of the visualized final pot in terms of form and depth. This is a little like finishing a painting in a frame.

The final pot does need to reflect the need of both these species for constant dampness. Shallow pots may be used if the soil is mounded and kept damp, but be vigilant! These trees reflect their woodland origin in their need of cool roots. In general terms, therefore, medium-deep containers are sensible if you are to avoid burnt leaves. Ele-

gant forms such as soft-cornered rectangles or ovals look well. Earth colours and muted glazes are desirable; and certainly avoid anything too shiny.

TABLE 1.2 *Feeding schedule*

Where several feeds are mentioned during the same period, alternate and space them at least one week apart.

Year 1 only: Follow Stage I feeding schedule but use Phostrogen at half strength once in June/July and use 0–10–10 at half strength once in August/September.

**Stage 1:** Years 2–5
Plants in development: seedlings, layerings, cuttings and collected trees that need mass. This schedule provides heavy growth and is used to build a tree quickly.

|  | TEF | Phos-trogen | Chempak no. 2 | 0–10–10 |
|---|---|---|---|---|
| January |  |  |  |  |
| February |  |  |  |  |
| March | 1 | 1 | 1 |  |
| April |  | 2 | 2 |  |
| May |  | 2 | 2 |  |
| June |  | 1 |  |  |
| July |  | 1 |  |  |
| August |  |  |  | 1 |
| September |  |  |  | 1 |
| October |  |  |  |  |
| November |  |  |  |  |
| December |  |  |  |  |

**Stage II:** Year 6 onwards:
Plants in structure and refinement.

|  | TEF | Phos-trogen | Chempak no. 2 | Osmocote | 0–10–10 |
|---|---|---|---|---|---|
| January |  |  |  |  |  |
| February |  |  |  |  |  |
| March | 1 | 1 | 1 | 1 |  |
| April |  | 1 |  |  |  |
| May |  | 1 |  |  |  |
| June |  | 1 |  |  |  |
| July |  | 1 |  |  |  |
| August |  |  |  |  | 1 |
| September |  |  |  |  | 1 |
| October |  |  |  |  |  |
| November |  |  |  |  |  |
| December |  |  |  |  |  |

## Feed analysis

|  | N | P | K |
|---|---|---|---|
| Phostrogen | 10 | 10 | 27 |
| Chempak no. 2 | 25 | 15 | 15 |
| Osmocote (3–4 month release) | 14 | 14 | 14 |
| 0–10–10 | 0 | 10 | 10 |

TEF 12% iron, 5% manganese, 4% zinc, 2% boron, 2% copper, 0.13% molybdenum.

## Feeding

### Phostrogen

This is a water soluble white powder. Useful also as a foliar feed. Generally available.
DOSAGE: 1 teaspoon per gallon and apply freely.

### Chempak no. 2

A blue powder, also water soluble. The high nitrogen content can be used to stimulate an early growth peak. Stocked by Chempak Products.
DOSAGE: 1 teaspoon per gallon and apply freely.

### Osmocote

A gold coloured, coated, granular feed from America. This is a slow release feed that gives a measured dose over 3–4 months and provides a background feed. Stocked by Chempak Products.
DOSAGE: 1 teaspoon per 25 cm (10 in) pot with 7.5 cm (3 in) depth.

### 0–10–10

A solution that is diluted to strength. This is both a flowering stimulant and growth hardener combined. 0–10–10 helps the plant overwinter safely and limits die-back. Stocked by Chempak Products.
DOSAGE: 1 tablespoon per gallon and apply freely.

### Trace Element Frit (TEF) 253A

A fine brown powder. It supplies all the micronutrients needed and one application lasts for a year. Stocked by Chempak Products.
DOSAGE: about $\frac{1}{2}$ teaspoon per pot.

Chempak Products, Geddings Road, Hoddesdon, Herts EN11 0LR

## Placement

As I have already indicated, light shade is sensible during hot summer weather as the leaves are easily burned. You must screen the trees from high winds, which can dry the soil and dessicate them very quickly. In winter I place my trees in a cold, well ventilated poly tunnel so that the fine twigs are not damaged by frost.

## Pests and diseases

Due to a change in government policy, some familiar insecticides have been withdrawn. Regretfully, I cannot suggest substitutes that have been tested over a reasonable period of time.

### Aphids

Round bulbous insects about 2 mm ($\frac{1}{16}$ in) in size. The types that infest Beech and Hornbeam trees are usually greyish.

*Symptoms* Blackish deposits of sooty, sticky honeydew on leaves. Shoot activity impaired. These pests appear throughout the growing season, or during a warm winter, or under glass. Quite mobile.

### Mealy bugs

Small oval insects about 1–2 mm ($\frac{1}{16}$ in) in size, covered in white fluffy wax.

*Symptoms* The appearance of fine white lint on leaves and shoots, causing that familiar general tired appearance.

# Production cycle over six years

## Development of mass:

### Raising by cuttings
*Appropriate for Hornbeams*

**Year 1**

Hardwood cuttings are taken in March and are prepared using either a straight or a wedge cut. Cuttings of around 7.5 cm (3 in) are a convenient size. They should be the width of a matchstick, or a little thicker. Prepare seed trays with an insertion mixture of 80% sand and 20% peat. Premoisten the container by immersing it in water and then tilt it to drain.

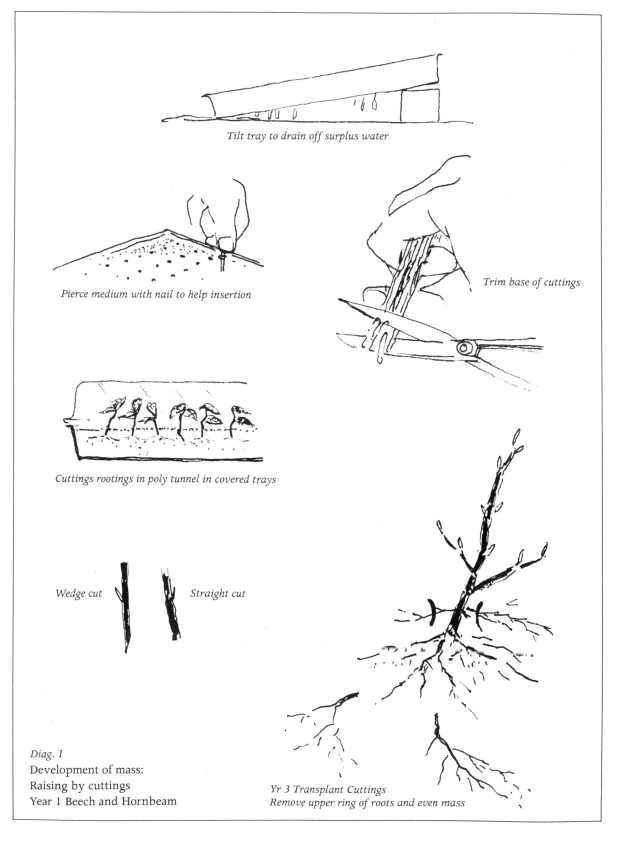

*Tilt tray to drain off surplus water*

*Pierce medium with nail to help insertion*

*Trim base of cuttings*

*Cuttings rootings in poly tunnel in covered trays*

*Wedge cut*　　*Straight cut*

*Diag. 1*
Development of mass:
Raising by cuttings
Year 1 Beech and Hornbeam

*Yr 3 Transplant Cuttings*
*Remove upper ring of roots and even mass*

You will need strong hormone powder to stimulate 360° of root initials. Insert the cuttings to a depth of 2.5 cm (1 in) and firm them in. Make sure the container is placed on blocks to encourage good air circulation. Spray periodically with Benomyl, or a similar fungicide. Remove any fallen leaves from the surface of the tray to alleviate root rot problems. Shade the trays and sprinkle the foliage as it opens, to maintain moisture levels in the cuttings. Place the trays under a slatted bench in a poly tunnel with good ventilation.

Cuttings of Hornbeam usually root in a rather random fashion, according to the vigour and condition of the donor source, so do not feed in Year 1. Some Vitamin B1 from time to time is helpful. Protect from frost during winter.

### Year 2

Allow the cuttings to grow without interference. Weak feeds of Phostrogen and 0−10−10 are beneficial but hold back until bud activity determines the live cuttings. If the response is ragged, hold back the feed and use Vitamin B1 until buds and shoots look stronger. Protect over winter.

### Year 3

The cuttings are transplanted in March as buds elongate. Spread the roots as radially as possible. If there is an upper and lower root system, as often develops with vigorous material, then choose the stronger, and remove the rival root ring. Tip back all strong roots to promote an even production of feeder roots throughout the new system. Use half trays or poly pots and fill them two-thirds full with soil. Place the spread root system and anchor with at least 2.5 cm (1 in) of soil. Water carefully and feed after one month. Protect over winter.

## Development of mass:

### Raising by seed

*Appropriate for Beech*

(*Note* − Hornbeams are faster than Beech from cuttings.)

### Year 1

Soak the seed and discard any that float. Seedlings are usually sown in March. Sow the seeds in trays containing a mixture of 3 parts clean sand to 1 of peat. Pre-moisten the trays prior to sowing and drain well. Use drills to ensure an even distribution of seed. Do not plant too close to the edge of the tray. Sow by individual placement and cover lightly with sandy soil. Raise the trays on blocks to encourage air circulation. (This is particularly important with large seeds that can easily rot with too much water.) Spray with fungicide periodically.

Seedlings should sprout in May. Spray with fungicide on emergence of the new cotyledons. Feed lightly during the first year. Once the seedlings have produced two or more sets of leaves, use a diluted feed of Phostrogen during June and July and a diluted feed of 0−10−10 in August and September. Keep in a poly tunnel and protect over winter.

### Year 2

Just as buds elongate transplant the seedlings and cut the tap root and longer roots. Spread the roots radially when planting. Aftercare is the same as for the cuttings. When feeding, follow the Feed Schedule for Year 2. Keep in a poly tunnel and protect over winter.

### Year 3

In spring transplant the seedlings into individual half trays or deeper poly pots, ensuring minimal root disturbance. In either case, greater root spread is beneficial. I usually add about 2.5 cm (1 in) of soil over the newly transplanted root area to keep it cool and to allow the major surface radials to gain body. Keep leaf sprayed over the growing season. Follow the procedures for Year 2 and spray for mealy bugs and other pests if necessary.

## Development of mass:

*Appropriate for both Hornbeam and Beech, and for both cuttings and seedlings*

### Year 4

*Placement*  In March move the young plants to a well lit, airy spot in the poly tunnel.

*Water*  Water well.

*Feeding*  Follow the schedule for Stage I.

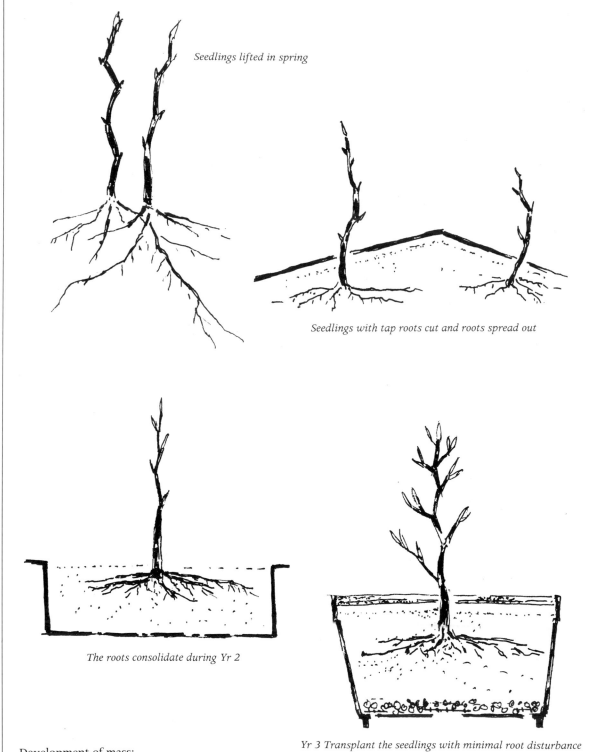

*Seedlings lifted in spring*

*Seedlings with tap roots cut and roots spread out*

*The roots consolidate during Yr 2*

*Yr 3 Transplant the seedlings with minimal root disturbance to deeper pots*

Development of mass:
Raising by seed
Year 2 Beech and Hornbeam

*Pests*   Spray as necessary.

*Shoot pruning*   Some pruning may be necessary in June to achieve a balanced and conical form. Try to be sparing in the pruning, however, as fast growth will build the plants rapidly.

*Branch pruning*   None.

*Wiring*   None.

*Protection*   Avoid frost contact and place on the floor of the poly tunnel early.

## Structure and form

### Year 5

*Placement*   Transplant the young plants in March. Trim the trunks back to stimulate side branching and to promote stocky stature. Cleanse the roots and remember to 'top and tail' the system as before, so that only one set of potential surface roots are kept. I find that it helps the species in their surface root development if a flat plate is placed under the main root system. The lack of direct plunging downwards has a highly desirable effect on trunk flare as the redirected roots strike out strongly sideways. Use full-sized seed trays at the very least. This will mean using a 'plate' about the size of a saucer.

*Water*   Water in using Vitamin B1 solution. After this be cautious over soil watering and apply only as buds open and the soil dries a little.

*Feeding*   Follow the schedule for Stage I after one month, usually at the end of April. Go straight on to Stage I feed schedule at full strength. I often supplement the schedule with a couple of tea-spoons of Osmocote.

*Pests*   Spray as necessary.

*Shoot pruning*   Trim the shoots in the upper half of the trees by 50% to keep taper. Allow full rein to all others.

*Branch pruning*   Remove unnecessary branches in autumn and seal the cuts.

*Wiring*   Trunks are wired in June.

*Protection*   Avoid frost contact and place on floor of poly tunnel.

*Note* – In my experience, both Hornbeam and

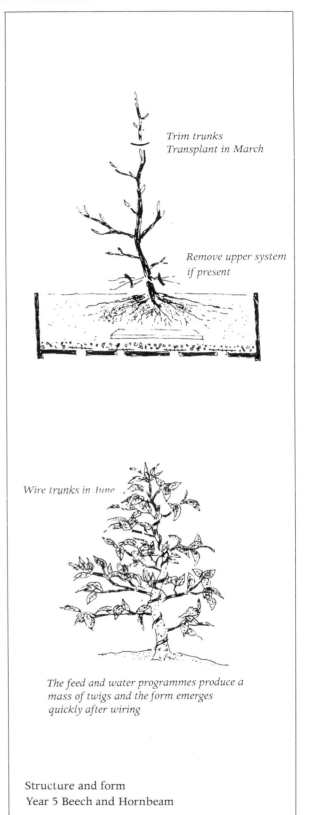

*Trim trunks*
*Transplant in March*

*Remove upper system*
*if present*

*Wire trunks in June*

*The feed and water programmes produce a mass of twigs and the form emerges quickly after wiring*

Structure and form
Year 5 Beech and Hornbeam

Beech can be developed very quickly if given plenty of food and water. I have frequently taken pieces of hedging Beech and Hornbeam material and have put a full branched system on them in a year by this method. As young trees tend normally to form basic branches in Years 4 and 5, this is an obviously useful technique to use. Contrary to popular 'Bonsai' belief, if high nitrogenous feeds and copious water are used you will have almost as many bud breaks as with a Maple!

## Refinement of image

### Year 6

*Placement*   Move to an area with good light inside the poly tunnel. Dewire the trunks in March.

*Water*   Water well.

*Feeding*   Change over to Stage II feed schedule for both species.

*Pests*   Spray as necessary.

*Shoot pruning*   Pinch the soft growth consistently.

*Branch pruning*   In mid to late summer any heavy branches are removed to encourage finer growth. Spur trim the branches in late season to preserve compact growth.

*Wiring*   Train branches after the removal of the heavy ones in mid to late summer.

*Protection*   Avoid frost contact and place on floor of poly tunnel.

Purchasing Hornbeams grown for hedging material was a good way of obtaining potential Bonsai in the fifties and sixties when imported trees were unknown.

I remember the look of anguish on one grower's face when I lopped off the heads of highly desirable, chunky specimens and asked for a discount on the redundant bit!

Field-grown trees will often produce fluting at the bole of the trunk, generated by the strong lateral root action. This effect can be enhanced or initiated by shortening the *depth* of the root mass as one transplants.

The other method of obtaining Hornbeams was, of course, by collecting and the problem was that whilst not uncommon, the local number of this species was often limited. I remember finding a cache of young trees that had seeded themselves into heavy clinker on a railway line. What trunks they had! The collecting process was of the stuff Bonsai dreams are made of: I simply rolled away the flints and clinker and discovered craggy, twisted trunks, where the seedlings had been sculpted as they grew round the stones. Some of the trees were even attached: root-over-clinker style!

The box, or deep growing bed, soon enhanced the hedging and the natural material alike. I found that where the trees were collected or dug from deeply loamy sites, the roots tended to go down in a prolonged, claw formation. When there was an impediment, the roots spread and webbed very nicely. This led me to the technique of cutting the roots in such a way as to preserve a thin vertical section. Temporary downward root-growth inhibitors such as roofing tiles or old plates placed under the main trunk enhanced the effects of lateral expansion. *Note* – It is important to provide good drainage when the roots are cut short to avoid root rot.

Collecting Beeches provided much the same type of challenge. Again, a lot of Beeches can be very shallow rooted; where they grow on chalk for example, it is always worthwhile investigating the depth of the root mass of even very large calibre trunks. Heavy trunked Beech are often found in abandoned and overgrown hedgerows. Look for silver bark and compact branches. Being so shallow rooted, Beech usually transplant easily, and I remember collecting a lot of small-size trees to form a group and was amazed at how rapidly they leafed out after quite major root disturbance.

I found it was important to ensure fast drainage with this species generally, no matter whether the source was cultivated or wild, and later found this requirement extended to the imported Japanese Beech and Hornbeam.

I remember two cases that demonstrate the need for fast drainage. The first tree was a Japanese Beech that had total branch collapse and which, on repotting into light soil, budded afresh from root to apex, and second, a Japanese Hornbeam that was dead on arrival in the UK through Phytopthera, a disease aggravated by heavy, wet soil condition. This second example was really heartbreaking as the tree was exquisitely proportioned and really old.

In mid to late summer unnecessary branches are removed or shortened

Branches are wired down after pruning

In Yr 7 the tree begins to emerge. Always thin out the twigs as my suggested feed and water programmes will make a very full tree

Refinement of image
Year 6 + Beech and Hornbeam

# Table 1:3  Summary chart of the development of Beech and Hornbeam Bonsai

| | | | |
|---|---|---|---|
| **Stage I** Development of mass | | | |
| | YEAR **1** | YEAR **2** | YEAR **3** |
| JAN | | Winter protection, keep just damp ⟶ | |
| FEB | | Winter protection, keep just damp ⟶ | |
| MAR | Insert Hornbeam cuttings. Sow Beech seed. Spray with Benomyl. | Cuttings should sprout, remove obvious dead ones. If budding is not general give Vit. B1 – if budding is strong give weak feeds of Phostrogen and 0–10–10. Transplant seedlings prior to budding if possible. | Cuttings are transplanted. Seedlings are transplanted. Use $\frac{1}{2}$ trays and spread roots. Sort out any twin root systems. |
| APR | Spray cuttings with Benomyl. Spray seed trays with Benomyl. Remove any fallen foliage from cutting trays. Give Vit. B1 to cuttings. | Maintain largely as for Yr 1 but seedlings may be fed following schedule for Stage I. $\frac{1}{2}$ strength after one month. | After one month both seedlings and cuttings may be fed following schedule for Stage I. $\frac{1}{2}$ strength. Maintain as for Yr 1. Keep damp. |
| MAY | Beech seedlings should sprout. Spray with Benomyl. Spray cuttings to maintain leaf moisture. | Keep moist. | Spray for aphids if necessary. Keep moist. |
| JUNE | Feed seedlings with Phostrogen. Spray cuttings to maintain leaf moisture. Remove any fallen foliage. | | |
| JULY | Feed seedlings with Phostrogen. Maintain cuttings with leaf spray and Benomyl. | | |
| AUG | Feed seedlings with 0–10–10. Maintain cuttings with leaf spray and Benomyl. | | |
| SEPT | Both cuttings and seedlings protected in poly tunnel. Keep damp. | Keep damp. | Keep damp. |
| OCT | | | |
| NOV | | | |
| DEC | | | |

| | Stage II<br>Structure and form | Stage III<br>Refinement of image | |
|---|---|---|---|
| YEAR 4 | YEAR 5 | YEAR 6 | YEAR 7 |
| Move to airy well lit part of poly tunnel. Follow feed schedule for Stage I at full strength. Spray for aphids if necessary. Water well. | Transplant plants. Prune trunks back to promote back buds and make stocky form. Sort out any malformed roots. Place plate under trunk zone. | Dewire trunks. Pinch growth constantly. Water well but change over to feed schedule Stage II. Spray for aphids. Water well. | Repot trees into 'final' pot. Dewire branches. |
| | After one month follow feed schedule for Stage I. Add Osmocote for fast development. Water well. Spray for aphids. | Water well. | After one month follow feed schedule for Stage II. Spray for aphids. Pinch growth constantly. Water well. |
| | | | Follow Yr 6. |
| Some pruning may be necessary to achieve balanced conical form. Not too much, as the extra growth fattens trunks. | Allow twigs in the lower half of the trunk to develop. Trim top half growths by 50% to keep taper. Wire trunks. | Heavy branches removed to encourage even, fine growth. Wire branches. Seal cuts. | |
| Continue March schedule. | Continue April schedule. | Continue March schedule. Prune trunks back to improve taper. | |
| Feed plants with 0–10–10 at 1 tablespoon per gallon water = $\frac{1}{600}$: this hardens growth. | Remove unnecessary lower branches. Seal cuts. Feed with 0–10–10. | Feed with 0–10–10 | |
| Feed plants with 0–10–10 for last time. Keep damp. | Feed plants with 0–10–10 for last time. Keep damp. | Spur trim branches to preserve compact growth. Feed with 0–10–10. Keep damp. | |

27

# 2 Profile on Elm and Zelkova

## Natural habitat and plant description

*Ulmus parvifolia*, the Chinese Elm, is a native of China and grows from mainland China and Taiwan to Korea. It is a smallish tree making up to 16 m (50 ft). The form is typically rounded and broom shaped. The two main cultivars used in Bonsai are the cork bark and smooth, silver bark varieties. Old cork bark trees display a deeply fissured, almost winged, deep brown bark. Growth habit of the young foliage is appealing, with pink buds turning into masses of tiny, yellow green leaves that sprout out vigorously. The cork and silver bark forms have differing leaf size: the leaf of the cork bark is bigger and often white-flecked in early spring. With trimming, the leaf of the silver bark cultivar will reduce down to less than 5 mm ($\frac{1}{4}$ in). Both Elms grow vigorously and hold their leaves in mild winters, when they become almost evergreen. The winter tracery of trunk, branches and fine twigs is beautiful: the cork bark resembling the warm darkness of an old Scots Pine and the silver bark, the ghost image of a mature Zelkova.

*Ulmus procera argenteovariegata*, the white variegated English Elm, is often a large tree of up to 30 m (90 ft). Typically Elm shaped, like a tall, elongated dome, this tree often appears in the hedges and suckers along the roadside. The bark is dark grey brown and cracked into tiny square sections. Foliage is typically Elm shaped and the colours are very attractive, ranging from grey white to white on dark green, and are either splashed or solid. The leaves are either obovate or rounded, and carry around ten or twelve pairs of veins. The growth of trunk, branches and shoots is rapid, and is wonderfully reduced in scale with Bonsai culture, without loss of vigour. Cultural methods are as for the Chinese Elm.

*Zelkova serrata* – in Bonsai jargon, the Grey Bark Elm – is a native of Japan. It is a smallish tree about the size of the Chinese Elm. The form is usually that of a wide spreading broom, broadly rounded.

Old trees develop bark of a deep silver grey, and

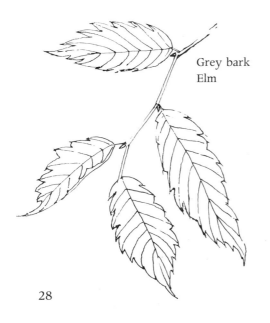

Grey bark Elm

Chinese Elm

White variegated English Elm

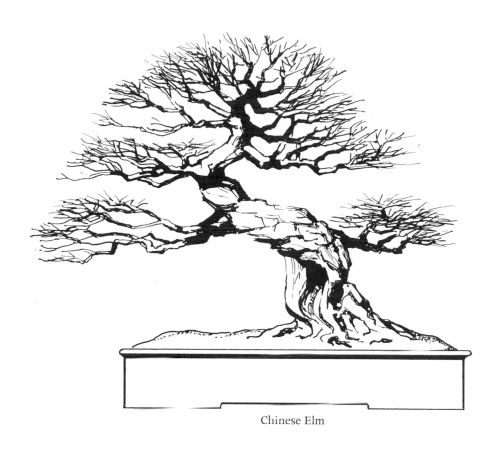

Chinese Elm

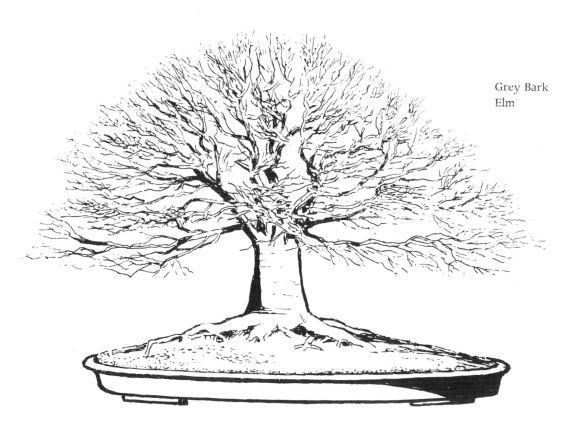

Grey Bark
Elm

29

are horizontally marked with orangy brown patterning of lenticels. The bark thickens and cracks away in flakes as the tree ages, leaving a light brown coloured bark reminiscent of the underbark of a Trident Maple.

Shoots are prolific and twist towards and away from each leaf, lending a kinked look to the arching growth. New shoots are reddish, the mature leaves dark green, and the autumn colour often a palette of deep yellows, reds and oranges. The leaf is lance-like, very saw edged and has eight to twelve pairs of veins. The winter image is perhaps the most popular with owners of Zelkova Bonsai, when the tree displays a mass of silvered twigs. Both Elms and Zelkovas give a true feeling of miniature trees through the fineness of their twig display.

# Horticultural preferences as Bonsai

## Soil

Elms need light soil because their roots are fleshy and very soft. If the soil is heavy, the British winter with its familiar patterns of rainfall and frost will alternately drown and freeze the roots until they rot.

A well composed sand consisting of some weathered but mostly rounded particles in a range of sizes between 2–3 mm ($\frac{1}{8}$ in) for the main soil, with 4–6 mm ($\frac{1}{4}$ in) for the lower soil and drainage course, seems to work well. As with Beech and Hornbeam, round sand produces a gently branched type of top growth that enables the grower to develop the fine twigs so admired in these species.

The second soil component is peat and long grained is best for water retention. The next component is leaf mould, well decomposed and sieved to remove both the ultra fine and any large leaves. Oak and Beech are the best. The last component is 'Arthur Bower's Ericaceous Compost'.

The final mixture is:

    4 parts sand
    2 parts peat
    2 parts leaf mould
    2 parts A.B.E.C.

Ensure all ingredients are dry and then combine them and sieve away the fines. The soil should feel light in the hands. If it appears to look very dark, another part of sand will improve the texture.

Zelkovas will also grow well in a soil that is heavier but it must be well drained. A heavier soil can ensure that greater moisture is available, thereby minimizing the risk of leaf scorch. Elms may also benefit in the same way from a slightly heavier mixture, but remember to protect the trees from heavy rain and winter weather. If the growing site is constantly exposed and windy, the use of the heavier mixture might be a good choice.

TABLE 2.1 *Water requirements of Elm and Zelkova*

**Stage I:** Plants in development. Generous watering encourages vigour.

| January | Damp |
|---|---|
| February | Damp |
| March | Moist |
| April | Moist |
| May | Moist |
| June | Moist |
| July | Moist |
| August | Moist |
| September | Moist |
| October | Damp |
| November | Damp |
| December | Damp |

**Stage II:** Plants in structure and refinement. Water is used to try and promote neater growth.

| January | Damp |
|---|---|
| February | Damp |
| March | Moist |
| April | Evenly damp |
| May | Evenly damp |
| June | Evenly damp |
| July | Evenly damp |
| August | Evenly damp |
| September | Evenly damp |
| October | Damp |
| November | Damp |
| December | Damp |

Plants in development need plenty of water to encourage top growth and trunk expansion. Make sure drainage is adequate and fast. Plants in structure and refinement need almost the same amount, especially in a heatwave, but not enough to encourage sappy growth. Foliage spray is beneficial.

## Water

Keep the Elm and Zelkova evenly damp. If there is any drought, the inner leaves will yellow and fall.

When developing these trees I find that it pays to place a plate or tile beneath the main trunk to spread the root mass. I followed the same principle at my nursery, which is sited on a hillside, by laying a black polythene sheet to limit downward root growth. I placed a deep layer of mixed peat and rotted pine needle directly on to the plastic in a series of raised beds. The Elms were planted directly into these beds and fed generously. There was a fast run-off of water and the trees produced heavy trunks as the tops and extending roots grew rapidly. Those Elms at the bottom of the bed naturally received the lion's share of food and water and their rapidly expanding root tips soon found their way off the edge of the plastic sheet. The combination of open growth with all the other factors produced trunks that expanded at 2.5 cm (1 in) a year.

Either in the beds or in large containers, I give enough water to spur strong growth. It is easy to judge the vigour by checking that the shoot growth is plump and that growth tips are brightly coloured. In containers on a growing bench where some semblance of order is required, give enough water to maintain healthy shoot production, but do not drown the trees. Evening foliage spray is very beneficial.

## Transplanting

### Standard repotting

Follow usual Bonsai procedures employing the suggested soil mixtures. First check the Elm for heavy roots and remove these if they dominate an otherwise even root pad. They may be planted as root cuttings and soon produce stocky little trees with gnarled trunks.

Even and thin out the root mass so that it spreads radially and sits well. I wash the root systems to judge better their structure and vigour. Often there will be lower roots that are more attractive than those above. The washing will show all this more clearly. Do not hesitate to remove undesirable or heavy roots. These can be converted to root cuttings. Often the trunk will throw out new surface roots in the trimmed area

and these can be incorporated with the newly exposed lower roots.

Sometimes, instead of removing a faulty surface root entirely, it may be severed at the trunk line and then elevated so the cut section sprouts as a root cutting, thus making another trunk. This step could be repeated more than once to make a root-connected group.

Zelkovas are very easy to repot and their roots are finer and not so touchy.

### Repotting frequency

Because Elms grow so fast below ground, repotting is vital at all stages. In the ground or in the raised beds, the trees were transplanted and retrimmed on a yearly cycle. In large containers every two years is often enough. In Bonsai containers, when the growth is more regulated, every two to three seasons is enough. Zelkovas are treated identically.

### The relationship of root pruning and branch pruning

Try always to preserve a balance above and below the soil line. As trees develop, the aim is towards finer and finer top growth, with the emphasis on taper and graceful form. Therefore, at repotting time, carefully consider the branches and remove any that do not contribute to the general feeling of airiness. Usually if you need to remove heavy roots, there will be more than one counterpart branch that needs to come off.

In restyling a large Chinese Elm for a friend, it was necessary to remove fully formed branches. These and all their attendant twiggery were far too beautiful not to try and save. Using a medium light insertion mix, each branch was base trimmed, hormone dipped and inside a month, had rooted and were on their way to becoming gorgeous small-sized Bonsai.

When a Broom Elm throws many branches from a common whorl, a large swelling will be encountered which in time on the lower trunk, for example, will lead to reverse taper. It is possible to split the trunk at repotting time and to open it to correct this fault. Later in the book I show such a broom Elm that I plan to operate on in this way.

Elms and Zelkovas (and incidentally, Hackberrys, Apples and Cedars) produce bulges around the bases of any branches that are vigorously grown. Also, when the trees are branch pruned in spring or in mid season, the same un-desirable 'football' calluses are formed.

I have discovered that if the offending portions are trimmed away at the end of the year they will heal flat. It is even possible, through this late pruning method, to pare down branches that are too heavy, although well placed, and so restore a balance of form. Remember to seal the cuts with Kiyonal (Japanese wound paint), in order to keep them moist and to protect them from frost. If branches must be removed in spring or in mid season, leave a generous stub and remove this at the recommended later time.

## Containers

The chosen container must act as a perfectly drained flower pot: both species are adversely affected by standing water, as they need rapid exchange of oxygen and water.

Plants in development benefit from the use of raised beds or large wooden containers. Try to arrange matters so that the box is long and broad and not less than 15 cm (6 in) deep. Plants that are being structured need to be related to a container appropriate to the eventual form. Plants in refine-ment require pots of precise form and colour.

The cork bark Chinese Elm looks well in unglazed pots in greys, buffs and reds. It also looks very good with muted glazes in blues, greens and off-whites. Both thin and watery, or thickish and trickly glazes suit the tree. Much the same applies to the silver barked Chinese Elm and the Zelkova, but a quiet texture is more harmonious.

The form is dictated by the mood of the plant. Often an Elm with a solid trunk can be enhanced by a rectangular deepish pot and a broom made more graceful, with a lower graceful line. In general terms the whole group of species looks well in soft contoured ovals and rectangles of shallow to medium depth.

TABLE 2.2 *Feeding schedule*

Where several feeds are mentioned during the same period, alternate and space them at least one week apart. Feed is not really applicable in Year 1; cuttings may benefit from some dilute feed with 0–10–10.

**Stage I:** Years 2–5

Plants in development: seedlings, layerings, cut-tings and collected trees that need mass. This schedule provides heavy growth and is used to build a tree quickly.

|  | TEF | Phos-trogen | Chempak no.2 | Osmo-cote | 0–10–10 |
|---|---|---|---|---|---|
| January |  |  |  |  |  |
| February |  |  |  |  |  |
| March | 1 |  | 1 | 1 |  |
| April |  |  |  |  |  |
| May |  |  |  |  |  |
| June |  |  |  |  |  |
| July |  | ½ |  |  |  |
| August |  | ½ |  |  | 1 |
| September |  |  |  |  |  |
| October |  |  |  |  |  |
| November |  |  |  |  |  |
| December |  |  |  |  |  |

**Stage II:** Year 6 onwards: Plants in structure and refinement.

|  | TEF | Osmocote | 0–10–10 |
|---|---|---|---|
| January |  |  |  |
| February |  |  |  |
| March | 1 | 1 |  |
| April |  |  |  |
| May |  |  |  |
| June |  |  |  |
| July |  |  | 1 |
| August |  |  | 1 |
| September |  |  | 1 |
| October |  |  |  |
| November |  |  |  |
| December |  |  |  |

## Feed analysis

|  | N | P | K |
|---|---|---|---|
| Phostrogen | 10 | 10 | 27 |
| Chempak no. 2 | 25 | 15 | 15 |
| Osmocote (3–4 month release) | 14 | 14 | 14 |
| 0–10–10 | 0 | 10 | 10 |

**TEF** 12% iron, 5% manganese, 4% zinc, 2% boron, 2% copper, 0.13% molybdenum.

# Feeding

## Phostrogen

This is a water soluble white powder. Useful also as a foliar feed. Generally available.
DOSAGE: 1 teaspoon per gallon and apply freely.

## Chempak no. 2

A blue powder, also water soluble. The high nitrogen content can be used to stimulate an early growth peak. Stocked by Chempak Products.
DOSAGE: 1 teaspoon per gallon and apply freely.

## Osmocote

A gold coloured coated, granular feed from America. This is a slow release feed that gives a measured dose over 3–4 months and provides a background feed. Stocked by Chempak Products.
DOSAGE: 1 teaspoon per 25 cm (10 in) pot with 7.5 cm (3 in) depth.

## 0–10–10

A solution that is diluted to strength. This is both a flowering stimulant and growth hardener combined. 0–10–10 helps the plant overwinter safely and limits die-back. Stocked by Chempak Products.
DOSAGE: 1 tablespoon per gallon and apply freely.

## Trace Element Frit (TEF) 253A

A fine brown powder. It supplies all the micronutrients needed and one application lasts for a year. Stocked by Chempak Products.
DOSAGE: about $\frac{1}{2}$ teaspoon per pot.
(Chempak Products, Geddings Road, Hoddesdon, Herts EN11 0LR)

# Placement

Both Elms and Zelkovas like good light, but light shade in hot weather is sensible. Remember inner leaves die easily. Never shade Chinese Elm in winter as this can lead to severe die-back. Keep frost free and place in winter shelter early as the fine tracery is easily damaged.

# Pests and diseases

Due to the change in government policy, some familiar insecticides have been withdrawn. Regretfully, I cannot suggest substitutes that have been tested over a reasonable period of time.

## Aphids

Round bulbous insects about 2 mm ($\frac{1}{16}$ in) in size. The types that infest these trees are usually greyish.

*Symptoms* Blackish deposits of sooty, sticky honeydew on leaves. Shoot activity impaired. These pests appear throughout the growing season, during a warm winter, or under glass. Quite mobile.

## Scale insects

Flat or rounded scales look like pods, and vary from 1 mm ($\frac{1}{16}$ in) to 2–3 mm ($\frac{1}{8}$ in) in size, depending on type. They are usually a brownish colour. The females produce white egg sacs. They are quite mobile.

*Symptoms* Leaves can yellow substantially in dappled areas. The scale will be found attached to the leaves. The larger types batten on to the twigs, branches and trunk. There may be some sooty deposits or slick, shiny areas like snail trails.

# Production cycle over seven years

## Development of mass:

### Raising by cuttings

As the viability of most Elm and Zelkova seed is notoriously variable, I prefer to raise all these trees by cuttings. This also has the advantage of shortening time and permitting the grower to strike quite sizeable material. You will remember the comments about rooting mature branches from an old Chinese Elm Bonsai.

### Year 1

Take sections of previous year's wood (Block A). Cuttings are generally the thickness of a matchstick, although heavier material of Elms will root readily. The old branches mentioned previously were the thickness of between, say, a pencil or finger. March is generally the best month. Material between 5–10 cm (2–4 in) in length is best taken at this season. Prepare seed trays with a mixture of 50% sand to 50% peat and pre-wet the mixture by standing the trays in water to almost the same depth. Wait until air bubbles stop and then drain well.

You will need hormone rooting powder that is

strong enough for the job: medium strength for cuttings the thickness of a matchstick, and strong for the heavier material. Recut the base of all material prior to the hormone dip and insert without delay. Insert to a depth of at least 2.5 cm (1 in) and firm in. Make sure, particularly when using heavy material, that it does not touch the bottom of the tray. Because Elm material is often soft and rots easily, space the material evenly and avoid contact with the container wall (the cuttings need lots of air).

Spray the tops of the cuttings with a suitable fungicide and shade the trays lightly. Ensure the trays are up on blocks for good air passage and enclose the cuttings under plastic for humidity, or place them in a poly tunnel.

Another advantage of taking dormant cuttings is that the terminal bud is intact, leading to the development of perfectly straight trunks. This is a good feature when developing broom style trees.

It is possible to take summer cuttings (Block B) of all these species when new growth has extended and the shoots bear five or six leaves. Pinch out the soft tips and proceed as described but use a weaker hormone powder. With either method, after about a month try a tentative test pull to check for rooting. Be gentle! When resistance is felt and when new shoot growth is evident, some weak 0–10–10 feed at two week intervals will prove beneficial. Remove all fallen leaves and those cuttings that don't make it. Spray with fungicide on a monthly basis. Stop feeding by August and keep in the greenhouse over winter. Make sure the cuttings remain just damp.

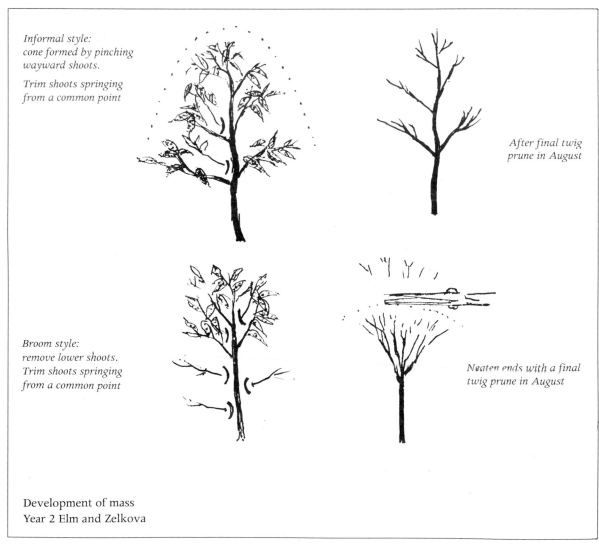

*Informal style: cone formed by pinching wayward shoots.*

*Trim shoots springing from a common point*

*After final twig prune in August*

*Broom style: remove lower shoots. Trim shoots springing from a common point*

*Neaten ends with a final twig prune in August*

Development of mass
Year 2 Elm and Zelkova

## Year 2

*Placement*  In spring, if cuttings bud back strongly they may be transplanted into individual 10 cm (4 in) pots. I use polypropylene pots and the recommended soil mixture for the species. Take time with the roots and spread them radially so the cuttings sit well. Remove any rampant roots completely and even up the others. Keep them protected in the greenhouse for this season.

*Water*  Water carefully and be cautious for the first few applications. Never let the cuttings dry out but do avoid drowning them. As buds pop out and leaves develop, water can be increased until it reaches normal levels.

*Feeding*  One month after transplanting, feed the cuttings according to the feed schedule for Stage I. However, if growth is slow, delay feeding and use Vitamin B1 instead until they pick up.

*Pests*  Use any sprays at half strength.

*Shoot pruning: Informal style*  From April to August trim wayward shoots to preserve or create an overall cone. Secondary buds spring strongly from leaf axils in response to the trimming and dense buds are soon formed. If larger trees are fancied, preserve a much larger cone. The key is to let lower branches grow strongly to thicken the trunk. Try not to let too many spring from one point as this will encourage a football-like callus to form. These knobs are very unsightly where trees are grown for tapered display, so remove excess shoots promptly. Two sprouts are fine and appear quite natural. Continue trimming through the summer and give a final twig prune in August. This leaves time for the plants to recover before the frost.

*Shoot pruning: Broom style*  If brooms are wanted, a reverse cone is created. Choose plants with straight trunks and rub low shoots away before they become woody. When branches form, allow only one at any point beside the extending trunk. Trim back when stronger branches exceed 10 cm (4 in) and reduce to 5 cm (2 in). Remove any sprouts that point in to the trunk and any that point straight down. In August neaten the ends by trimming with scissors. This creates a dome and reinforces the broomed form, as well as invigorating inner buds.

*Protection*  Place in an unheated spot in the greenhouse with good light. If placed on the floor, ensure there is air flow beneath the pots to prevent any standing water rotting the roots.

## Year 3: Informal style

*Placement*  Place the trees on elevated benches in the greenhouse when the buds start to open. This is the time to make your decision about the preferred eventual size. Normally you prune the trunk at the one-third point. So a trunk of 45 cm (18 in) in projected size, is pruned at 15 cm (6 in).

A great number of buds is created by this terminal pruning and two are selected to form the future trunk line and first branch. The pruning also helps the trunk to thicken. This reduction is repeated yearly using opposing branch patterns to make a zigzag. If tiny plants are wanted, by constantly thinning out the leaves, very dainty, fine branches are formed which blend well with the small trunks.

*Wiring*  Extending trunk lines may be wired to soften the straight lines if preferred. Check first to see the plants roots' are secure before wiring, to avoid injury by rocking to and fro. They should be well rooted by this time. If they are not, an extra year's feeding will provide additional root mass and should stabilize the trees.

*Water*  Be generous above and below as this encourages firm growth tissue.

*Feeding*  Follow the schedule for Stage I.

*Pests*  Spray as necessary.

*Shoot pruning*  Allow full rein to the extending trunk line until August and then reduce by half. Reduce the first branch by half after two months' growth, then keep it pinched for compact structure.

*Protection*  Place on the floor of the greenhouse or poly tunnel.

## Year 3: Broom style

*Placement*  Place on elevated benches in the greenhouse or poly tunnel when the buds start to open.

*Water*  Be generous above and below but make sure plants drain well.

*Feeding*  Follow the schedule for Stage I.

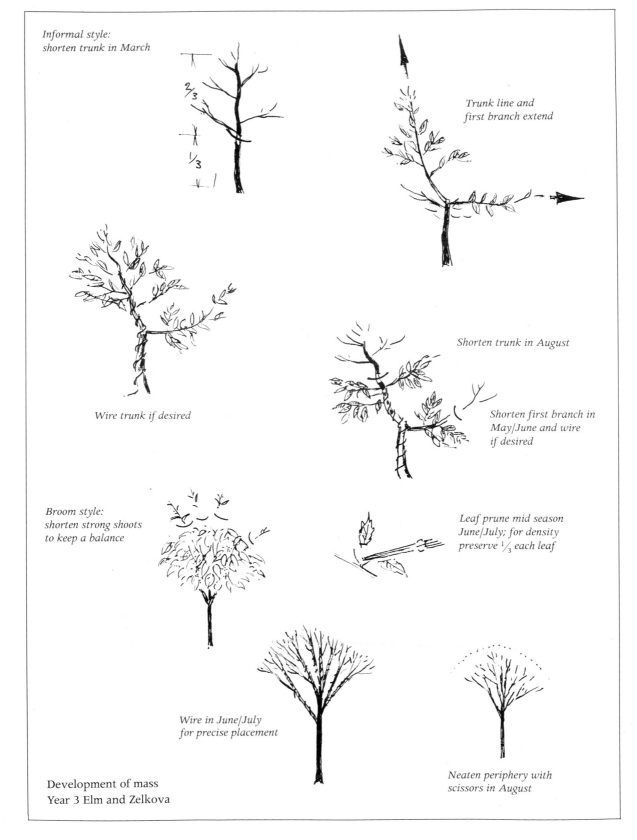

Informal style:
shorten trunk in March

Trunk line and
first branch extend

Wire trunk if desired

Shorten trunk in August

Shorten first branch in
May/June and wire
if desired

Broom style:
shorten strong shoots
to keep a balance

Leaf prune mid season
June/July; for density
preserve $\frac{1}{3}$ each leaf

Wire in June/July
for precise placement

Neaten periphery with
scissors in August

Development of mass
Year 3 Elm and Zelkova

*Pests*  Spray as necessary.

*Shoot pruning*  Trim back strong growths that threaten to dominate, and reduce them to 5 cm (2 in). Allow weaker shoots to extend to 15 cm (6 in), then trim back by half. This will preserve a balanced vigour. Never keep any heavy growths; always trim these off. Careful leaf and shoot trimming will force axillary growth and make the broom top full. Trim all inward facing shoots.

Around August, neaten the branch ends by gathering them up in one hand and using scissors to chop them back. I have used this technique on most species in the formative stages and it does provide a quick domed profile. Arguably, this chop can be made later to avoid football-like calluses forming. The choice of timing depends on where you live. If frosts come early to your area, for example, then make the cut in August. Trim any downward facing shoots and seal all cuts with Kiyonal.

*Wiring*  If the main potential branches are strong I coil them loosely with wire and bring them inwards to enhance the narrow upsweep, like the spokes of a half folded umbrella. This gives the chance to straighten and direct any limbs precisely. The alternative is to wrap all the limbs together and leave them tied over winter. I prefer loose wiring because it is a less random way to shape.

*Protection*  Make sure they remain frost free by placing in a poly tunnel.

### Year 4: Informal style

*Placement*  When the buds open, the trees are transplanted. They remain in the poly tunnel until the frosts are passed and are then placed on well-lit benches.

*Water*  After transplanting again, be careful about watering until the roots are established. Consider the trees as cuttings: keep the roots dampish and mist the leaves. When buds and shoots develop, slowly restore full watering.

*Feeding*  A month after transplanting, resume the schedule for Stage I.

*Pests*  Spray as necessary.

*Shoot pruning*  Follow the schedule for Year 3 and in addition make sure all new growth on the first branch is well pinched. In early spring, select the new trunk line and side branch formed by pruning in August Year 3. Make sure the new lines are on the opposite side so a zigzag trunk and outward flowing branches are created. Make sure the new trunk and branch terminating cuts are a little closer together than those made in Year 3. Seal cuts.

*Wiring*  Remove wire on trunks. Wire new trunk line and branches if desired.

*Protection*  Return to poly tunnel.

*Containers*  In Year 4 choose Bonsai containers that compliment the projected shape and size of the finished tree.

### Year 4: Broom style

*Placement*  When the buds open, the trees are transplanted. They remain in the poly tunnel until the frosts are passed and are then placed on well-lit benches.
*Note* – Take the greatest care in the placement of surface roots and the removal of roots that mar the outward flow of radial lines. Eliminate all heavy roots.

*Water*  As outlined in the **Informal** commentary, treat the young trees as cuttings until they are shooting strongly.

*Feeding*  A month after transplanting, begin the schedule for Stage II. The slightly less rich schedule will help monitor the fattening of the branch structure.

*Pests*  Spray as necessary.

*Shoot pruning*  Trim back all strong growth to encourage weaker shoots. Leaf pruning and soft pinching will promote rapid ramification of the broom structure. The key from now on is to shorten constantly or remove all shoots that go over 2.5 cm (1 in) in length. Neaten branch ends by late pruning, from August onwards depending on your frost zone. Thin out any whorls at branch tips and reduce to two.

*Wiring*  In early spring dewire all branches trained in the previous summer. In June and July loosely wire any new limbs intended for major placement in the design.

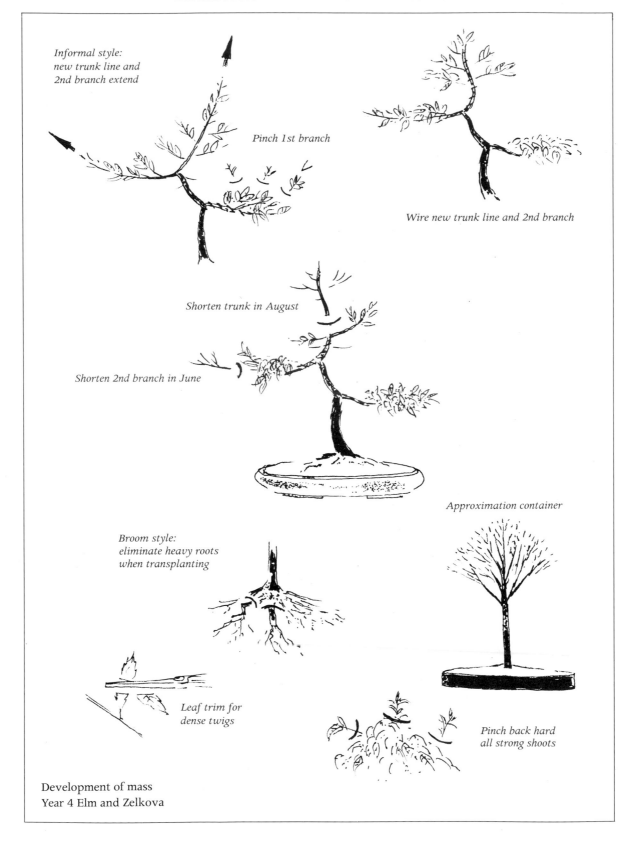

*Informal style:
new trunk line and
2nd branch extend*

*Pinch 1st branch*

*Wire new trunk line and 2nd branch*

*Shorten trunk in August*

*Shorten 2nd branch in June*

*Approximation container*

*Broom style:
eliminate heavy roots
when transplanting*

*Leaf trim for
dense twigs*

*Pinch back hard
all strong shoots*

Development of mass
Year 4 Elm and Zelkova

*Protection*  Place in the poly tunnel when frosts begin.

*Containers*  The time to choose the containers that will match the design is when transplanting the Broom trees. The cardinal rule with Brooms is to keep the roots cool for the next two seasons or so, in order that they may develop nicely to complement the top. Therefore, choose containers that are a little deeper than the aesthetic ideal so that the roots may be covered and develop well. Exposed, dry roots never develop well.

## Structure and form

### Year 5: Informal style
Largely a repeat of Year 4. Remove all wires. Continue pinching on the first and second branches to create pads.

### Year 5: Broom style
Largely a repeat of Year 4. Remove all wires. Pay minute attention to detailed pinching. Groom away inward facing and dropped shoots.

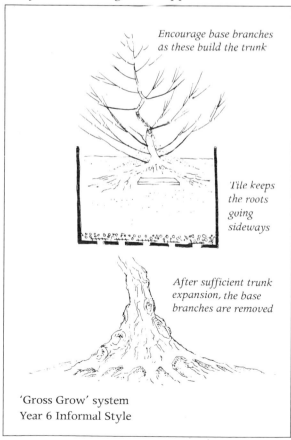

*Encourage base branches as these build the trunk*

*Tile keeps the roots going sideways*

*After sufficient trunk expansion, the base branches are removed*

'Gross Grow' system
Year 6 Informal Style

## Refinement of image

### Year 6: Informal style
In spring when the buds open, transplant the tree into a container of the desired form, *provided* the development of trunk girth is satisfactory and progressing according to the projected design. If it is not, then consider using large containers and 'gross grow' by providing a much larger environment. I still would not consider open ground if you wish to preserve the branches developed to date, as the feeding schedules I follow under these circumstances will coarsen and mar them. Instead I use custom-built wooden containers to give additional root run and growing area. Remember to place the container on blocks *before* filling with soil.

Remove all coarse roots and even the root mass. Place a plate or tile beneath the main trunk as the roots will grow very strongly and if channelled sideways, will increase the taper and thickness of the trunk quite dramatically in a very short time. Revert to feed schedule 1 and, in addition, feed with Osmocote. If the worst happens and the branch system looks too thick in relation to, or its position on the trunk, it may be removed and restarted. This is often standard procedure where branches are used purely to bodybuild the trunk and are later removed when the desired thickness is attained. Remember that Elms fatten quickly at branch junctions, so take full advantage for some adventurous Bonsai development. For example, try deep pruning back to a low branch and create amazing taper; its enormous fun! Make heavy cuts late in the season to avoid those football-like calluses forming and spoiling taper.

I suggest the best and most controlled results can be obtained if the trees are transplanted on a two year cycle. This gives time for sizeable increases in trunk diameter to develop and an opportunity to sort out any offending root and branch problems before they get too bad.

When replanting, recycle the soil by all means but add fresh 'Arthur Bower's Ericaceous Compost' and fresh leaf mould. Simply continue this system until the heaviness of the trunk is to your satisfaction. I produced an 8 cm ($3\frac{1}{2}$ in) trunk on a Black Pine in five years by this method. Chinese Elm grows up to three times as fast, and its neighbour, the Siberian Elm, even faster. Think about it!

The technique is worth trying on all the species in this book. I recall a Needle Juniper that was garden planted on the site of an old pig farm and produced a trunk that fattened at the rate of 2.5 cm (1 in) per year. The Beech, you will recall, and the very similar Hornbeam become as lively as Trident Maples with this treatment and trunks and branches are soon built. Chinese and Meyer's Juniper and Cryptomeria thrive on copious feed and water and unlimited root run.

Any wiring should be checked carefully and weekly. The wood fattens at an enormous rate and be prepared to cut away any wires that appear tight.

### Year 6: Broom style

Transplant into the container and proceed as for Year 5.

### Year 7: Informal style

Those trees of acceptable stature may be planted into their final containers. Keep them inside until frosts have passed, then place them outside.

*Water*  Be careful as always over the initial watering period, until bud activity picks up and indicates sound root growth.

*Feeding*  Begin feeding a month after root pruning. The objectives have now changed: the aim is to preserve taper and the emerging twig tracery, while keeping the foliage lively and green. You will find the combination of Osmocote, given as a light scattering in April, and applications of 0–10–10, given monthly at the recommended rate, will support but not spur the tree.

*Pests*  Spray as necessary.

*Shoot pruning*  Pinch all shoots to increase foliage density. Groom away inward and downward facing shoots and check that branch ends are not becoming heavy. Remove any knots of twigs at the end of the season.

*Protection*  Usual frost protection.

### Year 7: Broom style

Transplant the trees into their final containers and take special care with the roots, as some of the best surface roots may be exposed now. Keep the trees in the greenhouse till the frosts have passed, then place them outside.

Refinement of image
Year 7 + Elm and Zelkova

*Water*   Be careful not to overwater till there is overall bud activity.

*Feeding*   A month after transplanting follow the schedule for Stage II. The objectives for taper and fine tracery are even more important now, so if you experience strong growth, immediately cut the amount of feeding.

*Pests*   Spray as necessary.

*Shoot pruning*   Leaf trim the trees to promote extra fineness in the twigs. Check for and remove any of the faulty shoots.

*Protection*   Usual frost protection.

The search for exotics like Chinese Elm and Zelkova was really confined to specialized nurseries like Hilliers of Winchester, back in the fifties.

I vividly recall the thrill of seeing young Zelkovas grown as landscape plants way too big for my then-appreciation of chop-down techniques. As I remember it, the interest in Chinese Elm, or 'Nire' as the first importers styled it, did not really 'take off' until the early sixties, when cute little trees with heavy cork bark and tiny leaves appeared on the market. Even back then, by comparison the Zelkova, always styled 'Grey Bark Elm', was very expensive for anything halfway towards specimen status.

The beauty of these species from the propagation angle is their very fast development when taken as cuttings. In the early days, most people, myself included, wasted time with seeds and it was not till I equipped myself with a proper greenhouse and mist system that I seriously considered taking cuttings. The advantages are enormous of course, and I marvel at the prodigal waste of time prior to this, but in those days even a poly tunnel was considered dangerously *avant-garde* in Bonsai circles. I remember preaching the gospel of 'use your greenhouse as part of your tool kit' to a singularly unreceptive bunch of students! They all use them now I notice!

Playing with cuttings soon suggested the techniques of taking 'bunch-cuttings' or whorled sections, that quickly gave a group or cluster effect. As a lateral progression, I tried assembling cuttings in the pre-rooted stage, as groups – then later, I planted them close together through a plate that was slotted. This proved a major breakthrough! The cuttings fattened as they grew and grafted together! There was a massive callus that soon threw out masses of roots and the whole process enabled me to produce Clumps and Rafts and all manner of exciting small groups. The plates were removed at an early stage and the lateral roots encouraged to break strongly sideways. This produced trunks with flare of the sort that takes years to develop. The whole image of fused trunks and strong, outer trunk/root junctions, was very encouraging and I went on to use the system with the other species mentioned in this book, and then with Maples, Larch and even Pines!

Another technique that evolved from handling large numbers of Elms each year was the development of root-connected groups by exploiting the natural suckering habit of this species. I found, by accident, (the best, and indeed, the only teacher in those days!) that if certain Zelkova types were allowed lateral root run as a group within a Bonsai pot, that heavy trunk shortening of the dominant tree, in particular, generated a mass of shoots from the coiled, surface roots. Again, the ways in which this technique can be applied are enormous in number and entertainment value. The prerequisites appeared to be: that no tree or trees to be pruned hard were ever short of fertilizer, the more the merrier; and that no great time span of seasons was allowed after the group became root-bound before the 'chop' was made, to avoid a moribund condition setting in.

The Zelkova species I found to sucker regularly, and which made a good group generally, was *Z. carpinifolia*, the Caucasian Zelkova. Remember to make the cuts early in the evolution of the tree. If you delay and cut into older wood, problems of football calluses will arise. I suggest that the later pruning around September–October should still provoke the basal shoots in the following year. This would avoid the bulges in the trunk. What the budding rate would be I have no accurate idea as I have not practised this deep reduction technique on older stock in the latter half of the year.

# Table 2:3  Summary chart of the development of Elm and Zelkova Bonsai

| | | | |
|---|---|---|---|
| **Stage I**<br>**Development of mass** | | | |
| | YEAR 1 | YEAR 2 | YEAR 3 |
| JAN | | Keep damp and protected ⟶ | |
| FEB | | Keep damp and protected ⟶ | |
| MAR | Take cuttings of previous year's wood. Insert them and spray with Benomyl. Keep damp. Place in poly tunnel. Ventilate. Block A. | Transplant strong budding cuttings. Spread roots radially. Water carefully. Keep damp. Keep in ventilated poly tunnel. | Place both Informals and Brooms on elevated benches in the poly tunnel. For Informal: prune trunks to $\frac{1}{3}$ preferred size. Seal cuts. Wire trunk line if liked. Water well. For Broom: just allow to grow for now. Spray for aphids. Water well. |
| APR | Spray with Benomyl. Ventilate. | After one month feed following Schedule 1. If growth is uneven or weak do not feed, use Vit. B1. Check and spray for aphids $\frac{1}{2}$ strength. | Feed following schedule for Stage I for both types. Water well. Spray for aphids. For Broom: Reduce strong growth to 5 cm (2 in). Allow weak growth to reach 15 cm (6 in) then shorten. Do not prune Informal. |
| MAY | Take soft cuttings. Insert them, pinch out soft tips. Spray with Benomyl. Keep damp. Place in poly tunnel. Ventilate. Block B. | Pinch growth to create a cone. Check and spray for aphids. | Repeat April care. |
| JUNE | Test pull Block A. When resistance is general and new growth is pushing, feed with dilute 0–10–10. Ventilate. Keep damp. | For Informal: maintain Apr/May care. Also for Broom: simplify branches by removing excess buds. Trim back from 10 cm (4 in)–5 cm (2 in). Remove down pointing buds. | If small trees are wanted of Informal shape, the side branch may be shortened and pinched back for compact growth. Otherwise repeat April care. Seal cuts. |
| JULY | Spray with Benomyl. Test pull Block B and proceed as for June. Remove fallen foliage. | For Informal: maintain Apr/May care. Also For Broom: Repeat June care. Simplify branches by allowing only one to form at any point on the trunk. | Repeat April Care. |
| AUG | Stop feeding. Keep damp. | Feed with 0–10–10 at 1 tablespoon per gal. of water ($\frac{1}{600}$). Neaten branch-ends of both Informal and Broom by a final twig prune. Try to dome the Broom contours. | Feed 0–10–10. For Informal: reduce trunk extension by 50%. Seal cuts. For Broom: neaten branch ends with scissors. Try to make a dome. Trim downward and inward facing shoots. Seal cuts. |
| SEPT | | Stop feeding. Keep damp. | Stop feeding. Keep damp. Wire Broom branches for fine placement. |
| OCT | | | |
| NOV | | | |
| DEC | | | |

| | Stage II<br>Structure and form | Stage III<br>Refinement of image | |
|---|---|---|---|
| YEAR 4 | YEAR 5 | YEAR 6 | YEAR 7 |
| Transplant both types, take the greatest care to arrange the surface root radially, eliminate heavy roots. For Informal: choose new trunk and side branch lines. For both, after transplanting, wait till frosts have passed, then place outside. Water carefully. Remove wire. | Apart from the transplanting, Yr 5 is largely as for Yr 4 care. The main difference is in the pruning which is more detailed. Remove wires. Place outside. | For Informal: Transplant out into container, OR, gross-grow the tree in a large container for extra bulk. For Broom: transplant into containers. Proceed as for Yr 5. | Trees of acceptable stature may be transplanted into the final containers. Be careful with initial watering. |
| After one month feed Informal Schedule Stage I; feed Broom Schedule Stage II. Water carefully. Pinch & shorten Brooms to promote twigginess. Pinch first branch on Informal. Spray for aphids. | | If Informal trees are to be gross-grown, one month after transplanting, revert to feed schedule Stage I. Do not pinch expanding trunk and branches until Aug. | One month after transplanting give a light feed of Osmocote and a feed with 0–10–10. Keep evenly moist. Pinch foliage carefully. Watch for aphids. |
| Repeat April care. | | | Feed with 0–10–10. Keep moist. Spray for aphids. Pinch foliage. |
| | | Feed with 0–10–10. | |
| Follow August Yr 3. For Informal: ensure the trunk and side branch terminating cuts are shorter than Yr 3. Seal cuts. For Broom: neaten branch ends with scissors. Reduce terminals and knots to two. | | Reduce lines of main branches and trunk extensions by 50%. Leave stubs to clean off later. Seal cuts. Repeat this each year until girth is satisfactory. | |
| Stop feeding. Keep damp. Place in poly tunnel. | | Stop feeding. Keep damp. All gross grown trees leave in containers outside. All trees in Bonsai pots, into winter location. | |
| | | When leaves drop clean off large stubs and re-seal. | |

*In March, for Brooms, choose containers a little deep to keep roots cool and developing well. For Informals, choose containers of approximately the projected size.

43

# 3 Profile on mixed Juniper species and Cryptomeria

## Natural habitat and plant description

*Cryptomeria japonica*, the Japanese Cedar, is a native of Japan and some parts of China. It is a fair-sized tree, often making 35 m (114 ft). The form is neat and usually compact, rounded and round topped. The lower branches may sweep down. The overall impression is similar to that of the Giant Redwood.

The mature bark is fibrous and reddish and the trunk is often fluted with age. There is often a wide-spreading root bole and flared trunk. The needles are vivid green and are quite broad and soft in section, whilst otherwise resembling the awl-like foliage of Juniper and Redwood. In damp conditions the tree will often produce vigorous annual growth. The shoots grow rapidly and inner activity is soon shed; hence the sparse look of old trees.

*Juniperus chinensis*, the Chinese Juniper, is native to China and Japan. It makes a medium-sized tree in ideal conditions, 18 m (59 ft), with a similar appearance to a well grown Cypress.

The bark is dark brown and stringy, often peeling away in strips. In many cases, the bark is twisted in form and the trunk is fluted. The foliage is a mixture of gorse-like needles and smooth, thin adult growth. The foliage is borne in compact layers on old trees. In younger plants, the end growths are plumose and vigorous, giving a tail-like appearance to each spray. Leaf colour varies from deep green through blue green, to light yellow green according to strain.

*Juniperus rigida*, the Needle Juniper, is native to Japan and Korea. It is a small tree, sometimes making 10 m (32 ft). The form is variable and akin

Chinese
Juniper

Needle
Juniper

Meyer's
Juniper

Japanese
Cedar

Japanese
Cedar

to Common Juniper in the way it can sprawl or remain upright. The foliage hangs down in sprays and is gorse-like, blue green and with a white central band down each leaf. Each leaf is itself fairly flexible, which is more than can be said for the points, from which it earns the name Needle Juniper! The bark is grey brown and inclines to peel away on older trees.

*Juniperus squamata meyeri*, Meyer's Juniper, is a shrub that is native to China. In Britain, it does well and sometimes reaches 8 m (26 ft). The plants soon form open, sprawling shapes, with plumose tips and lower branches that are open and weak. As young plants the growth is even and dense. The foliage is gorse-like and is a deep blue green with a central blue white stripe. As the foliage ages it clings on as a light brown scaled cladding along twigs and branches. The bark is deep brown and flaky and the trunks often have a fluted form as they age.

# Horticultural preferences as Bonsai

## Soil

Junipers and Cryptomerias do well in sandy soil. Junipers particularly are mountain trees preferring cloud cover and rapidly draining 'feet'. They have evolved in areas where mists and dew cover them and where their roots were set in rocks or mountain scree. Cryptomeria is an upland tree and does well with cloud cover and good drainage.

Both groups prosper in open soil, and in the collecting and establishing of Junipers, the use of high sand mixtures is a key factor to success. For over twenty years I have imported both groups from Japan and have always noticed that the trees with the best roots are grown in a mix with at least 70% fine river sand. The sand to use is the usual

Chinese Juniper

Chinese Juniper

one I recommend: a mixture of sharp and round particles in 2–4 mm ($\frac{1}{16}$–$\frac{1}{8}$ in) size for the main soil and 4–6 mm ($\frac{1}{8}$–$\frac{1}{4}$ in) for the lower soil and drainage course.

Added to this I use peat and leaf mould. Usually a ratio that works well is:

7 parts sand
1 part peat
2 parts leaf mould

If the 70%/30% ratio seems too sandy, add a little extra leaf mould.

TABLE 3.1 *Water requirements of Juniper and Cryptomeria*

| January | Damp |
|---|---|
| February | Damp |
| March | Moist |
| April | Moist |
| May | Moist |
| June | Moist |
| July | Moist |
| August | Moist |
| September | Damp |
| October | Damp |
| November | Damp |
| December | Damp |

## Water

Generally speaking, the chart explains the needs of all Junipers. A vital additional ingredient, central to the robust health of Junipers, is daily foliar misting, which supplies the 'cloud cover' so appreciated by this species. This also applies to Cryptomeria.

As I explained in *Bonsai Design: Scots Pine, Common Juniper and Japanese Larch*, in the section on Common Juniper culture, the correct use of water in conjunction with an open soil will quickly help Junipers and Cryptomerias flourish. It is important to shade Junipers and Cryptomerias to conserve leaf moisture and so ensure that new growth becomes sturdy and able to respond to the constant pinching that is necessary. Junipers and Cryptomerias that are foliage dry, for whatever reason, are soon subject to die-back and a generally miserable appearance, with extensive yellowing of the leaves. Desiccation may occur and this may be tested for by rolling the foliage in the

fingers: if it is brittle there is, or has been, insufficient water content in the plant. By shading, increasing humidity and by misting the leaves, this condition can often be improved. Sometimes the improvement will become apparent in the deepening colour of existing foliage, or sometimes in the production of new green buds from inner growing points. In most cases the yellowed leaves will drop.

If the tree is root bound there is always likely to be a problem in maintaining a proper moisture balance in the plant. This is aggravated if the tree is accidentally kept in a sunny position for any length of time, because when the roots become hot the foliage will be scorched as a result.

The Chinese, Meyer's and Needle Junipers and Cryptomeria, all enjoy regular foliage spraying. Chinese Juniper and Meyer's Juniper like plenty of soil watering too. Cryptomeria and Needle Juniper need less.

## Transplanting

The Chinese and Meyer's Junipers and Cryptomeria, are all easy to repot. The Needle Juniper, as it ages, can be slow to make new root, so the use of an humidity area like a poly tunnel is particularly desirable for this species for post-operative care. The other species, of course, also appreciate humidity. Be careful to provide good airflow at the same time.

### Repotting frequency

Chinese and Meyer's Juniper are repotted every two to three years; Needle Juniper every four and Cryptomeria, between two and four years according to vigour and age.

### The relationship of branch pruning and root pruning

It is important with all Junipers and Cryptomerias to repot at the specified periods to prevent a root-bound condition. With older and weaker trees, check for this by removing the tree from the pot. If there is a great number of roots on the outside of the root mass, it is time to repot. If not, it is safer and best to leave well alone. As I said in the previous section, the condition to avoid is when the roots cannot absorb sufficient water due to overcrowding.

At the time repotting becomes necessary, the foliage is usually dense. As the roots are thinned,

47

so it is vital to thin the foliage to admit light and air. At repotting time the two operations preserve the balance above and below. In addition to this, all these species benefit from regular foliage thinning. The additional light and air flow promote strong new growth. If thinning is not done and the repotting is delayed, die-back will occur.

At one time I had no less than a dozen specimen Junipers of various species brought in to me for reviving. They all had problems above and below. In every case they were old imported trees growing in heavy soil. The roots were coiled, crowded and the inner mass had felted up and rotted. The outer roots displayed some live tips but that was all. The top growth had degenerated to a mirror image of the root condition with meagre, hard little growth tips that displayed no extension, and with dead interior portions.

By root pruning, branch thinning and using lighter soil, along with the poly tunnel as a background humidifier, I was able to save and bring all the trees back to health. It took in some cases up to three seasons, but eventually they all went back to their owners looking green and perky.

The process of branch thinning entails the removal of dense inner growth. This is every bit as important as preventing branches overgrowing their length. It also allows you to groom and style in great detail, and adds quality as a result. This thinning and styling combination is fine on healthy trees, but if the tree is at all weak, simply thin it out.

## Containers

The Juniper is among the most flexible of subjects for training into, and collecting in, almost any conceivable shape. The form of the container therefore is dictated pretty much by the dynamics of the plant. Nothing too shallow is the general rule and medium depth ovals and rectangles look well with informal trees. With craggier trees, something deeper and rougher in texture will suit. Junipers make good cascades, so endless fun can be had figuring out what aspect to echo in the pot: sometimes the geometry, sometimes the curving trunk quality. Colours are important too and dull toned reds, browns, greys and neutrals are best.

Cryptomeria are grown as formal trees in singles, multiples or in groups, and ovals and rectangles usually work well. They may be soft or hard in outline to blend with the feel of the tree.

The same colour range applies. Sometimes it is fun to use a pale colour – even a glaze. Don't overdo the contrast. One or two in a collection is enough!

With either species and whatever the choice, the picture frame aspect is of secondary importance to that of the flower pot. It *must* drain well.

TABLE 3.2 *Feeding schedule*

Where several feeds are mentioned during the same period, alternate and space them at least one week apart.

**Stage I:** Years 1–5
Plants in development that need bulk. The schedule spurs heavy growth and is used to build a tree quickly.

| | Phostrogen | 0–10–10 | TEF | Chempak no.2 | Osmocote |
|---|---|---|---|---|---|
| January | | | | | |
| February | | | | | |
| March | | | 1 | 1 | 1 |
| April | 1 | | | 2 | |
| May | 1 | | | | |
| June | 1 | | | | |
| July | 1 | | | | |
| August | 1 | | | | |
| September | $\frac{1}{2}$ | 1 | | | |
| October | $\frac{1}{2}$ | | | | |
| November | | | | | |
| December | | | | | |

**Stage II:** Year 6 onwards:
Plants in structure and refinement.

| | Phostrogen | 0–10–10 | TEF | Osmocote |
|---|---|---|---|---|
| January | | | | |
| February | | | | |
| March | | | 1 | 1 |
| April | 1 | | | |
| May | | | | |
| June | | | | |
| July | | | | |
| August | | 1 | | |
| September | | | | |
| October | | | | |
| November | | | | |
| December | | | | |

## Feed analysis

|  | N | P | K |
|---|---|---|---|
| Phostrogen | 10 | 10 | 27 |
| Chempak no. 2 | 25 | 15 | 15 |
| Osmocote (3–4 month release) | 14 | 14 | 14 |
| 0–10–10 | 0 | 10 | 10 |

**TEF** 12% iron, 5% manganese, 4% zinc, 2% boron, 2% copper, 0.13% molybdenum.

# Feeding

### Phostrogen

This is a water soluble white powder. Useful also as a foliar feed. Generally available.
DOSAGE: 1 teaspoon per gallon and apply freely.

### Chempak no. 2

A blue powder also water soluble. The high nitrogen content can be used to stimulate an early growth peak. Stocked by Chempak Products.
DOSAGE: 1 teaspoon per gallon and apply freely.

### Osmocote

A gold coloured, coated, granular feed from America. This is a slow release feed that gives a measured dose over 3–4 months and provides a background feed. Stocked by Chempak Products.
DOSAGE: 1 teaspoon per 25 cm (10 in) pot with 7.5 cm (3 in) depth.

### 0–10–10

A solution that is diluted to strength. This is both a flowering stimulant and growth hardener combined. 0–10–10 helps the plant overwinter safely and limits die-back. Stocked by Chempak Products.
DOSAGE: 1 tablespoon per gallon and apply freely.

### Trace Element Frit (TEF) 253A

A fine brown powder. It supplies all the micronutrients needed and one application lasts for a year. Stocked by Chempak Products.
DOSAGE: about $\frac{1}{2}$ teaspoon per pot.

Chempak Products, Geddings Road, Hoddesdon, Herts EN11 0LR

# Placement

All the species like a well ventilated spot with light shading. The balance of water, shade and feed should be judged carefully. It is fairly easy to see if your local situation is adequate: the depth of blue green in the foliage, along with strong shoots, are obvious and reliable references. It bears repeating that all this group are easily burnt in the sun or scorched when rootbound.

Sometimes when plants are grown in full sun they will have a yellowish cast, and this is a look that is unacceptable in trees used for exhibition, because one is conditioned into identifying blues and greens as indicators of health and beauty. To restore this colour one has only to shade the trees for a few weeks.

I often grow these species in a poly tunnel after they have been transplanted or have undergone major restyling, as the humidity helps alleviate any stress. Be careful to move these species into their winter quarters early. They are often adversely affected by frost, *particularly* those trees that are heavily wired. In every case of winter kill over the years, I have found tight or heavy wire to be the cause when the plant is left out in the frost.

# Pruning variations

Chinese Juniper prefers light, soft tip pinching. Use the *soft* part of the thumb and forefinger to grip the foliage. If you have to go deeper than this: ie, if to catch the tip you have to use fingernails, you have not waited for sufficient growth extension. You will need about 1.25 cm ($\frac{1}{2}$ in) of growth for a safe margin. If deeper soft pruning is carried out, needle growth will be triggered. Adequate feeding and watering will help counteract the production of this type of growth. Do not trim it away too soon, as it will only return. Wait first for smooth adult foliage to reappear.

When scissors are used in grooming, cut only brown wood. When thinning and lightening trained branches, remove all inner shoots that clutter branch and twig junctions. Remove all lower growth that hangs below trained branch lines.

As the tree develops, with pinching it tends to assume a rounded section. Periodically, therefore, it is a good idea to thin out the denser areas and trim and wire sideways to lighten and flatten the forms. If this process is not carried out regularly the tree will soon sulk and lose vigour. Both heavier and lighter branches will choke and die back extensively.

Meyer's Juniper prefers light, but constant, soft

tip pinching. Use the soft part of the thumb and forefinger once again. The difference with Meyer's is that deep pinching is quite harmless. There is such a rapid build up of shoots when adequate feeding and watering schedules are followed, that scissor thinning to remove excess vertical height on branch planes has to be done on a regular basis, together with soft tip removal. Thin the inner growths to avoid pile ups of shoots that resemble knots. The inner shoot removal also helps the display of the lower branch and twig structure, so is more important to the design. Remove all old discoloured brown leaves. Thin out and style as for the Chinese Juniper.

Needle Juniper likes to expand vigorously and needs constant pinching. Preserve about 5 mm ($\frac{1}{4}$ in) of shoot and about three to four leaves if possible. You must remember to clean out ageing and dense foliage, in order to admit light and air to the interior areas. This entails using scissors to lighten and groom away excessive knots of shoots developed from previous pruning. Unless this method of thinning is practised, the tree will probably die back quite severely.

When thinned, pruned, fed and watered according to the schedule, the tree is very active and grows fast. Trees that are not pruned go yellow and develop arching branches that dangle weakly.

Cryptomeria appreciates soft tip removal of its foliage, using fingers whenever possible. It becomes very dense and, like the Junipers, it needs periodic thinning and cleaning to stay hyperactive. Traditionally scissors and Cryptomeria are said to be incompatible. The truth is, if metal is used on brown wood and fingers on the soft green, then all is fine. Any tearing, bruising or clipping across the foliage, by whatever means, will inevitably create yellowed foliage and brown ends that will need picking off. Groom and thin with scissors late in the spring (around May is a good time) and take out old wood. Soft pinch with fingers all through the season. Avoid slashing through overgrown green shoots. It is better to prune deeper into old wood and use the resultant dwarfer, soft shoots.

All the species discussed appreciate a rest in a poly tunnel after thinning and styling. Plenty of foliage spray and a good feed with Chempak no. 2 (high nitrogen) will soon have the trees recovered and responsive. Never put them straight back in full sunlight or they will dry up and die back for sure.

## Pests and diseases

Due to the change in government policy, some familiar insecticides have been withdrawn. Regretfully, I cannot suggest substitutes that have been tested over a reasonable period of time.

### Aphids
Round bulbous insects about 2 mm ($\frac{1}{16}$ in) in size. The types that infest these trees are usually greyish.

*Symptoms* Blackish deposits of sooty, sticky honeydew on leaves. Shoot activity impaired. These pests appear throughout the growing season, or during a warm winter, or under glass. Quite mobile.

### Cryptomeria blight
Cryptomerias sometime get reddened areas of foliage in excessively wet conditions. This can be triggered if the soil is too heavy and generates a lot of humidity. I have found in the bad old days when one could buy copper fungicide, that this really took care of the problem. Do not confuse the rust red of blight for the purply colour that Cryptomerias can get over winter.

### Red spider mites
Tiny red spider-like insects. They appear during warm spring/summer months when the weather is dry.

*Symptoms* Bronze to greyish tinge that spreads on leaves. Leaves often fail to regain colour, or take many months to do so.

### Scale insects
Flat or rounded scales that look like pods, and vary from 1 mm ($\frac{1}{16}$ in) to 2–3 mm ($\frac{1}{8}$ in) in size, depending on type. They are usually a brownish colour. The females produce white egg sacs. They are quite mobile.

*Symptoms* Leaves can yellow substantially in dappled areas. The scale will be found attached to the leaves. The larger types batten on to the twigs, branches and trunks. There may be some sooty deposits or slick, shiny areas like snail trails.

# Production cycle over six years

## Development of mass:

*Appropriate for cuttings and small nursery stock of Chinese, Meyer's, Needle Juniper and Cryptomeria*

### Year 1

In March select plants of two to three years that have a compact bushy form. Trunks should be no more than the thickness of a pencil to take standard wiring techniques. Formers and clamps may be used on heavier trunks, or these may well be sculpted down to the chosen size and form. There is a very good example of this technique illustrated in the case history of tree no. 4, a Meyer's Juniper.

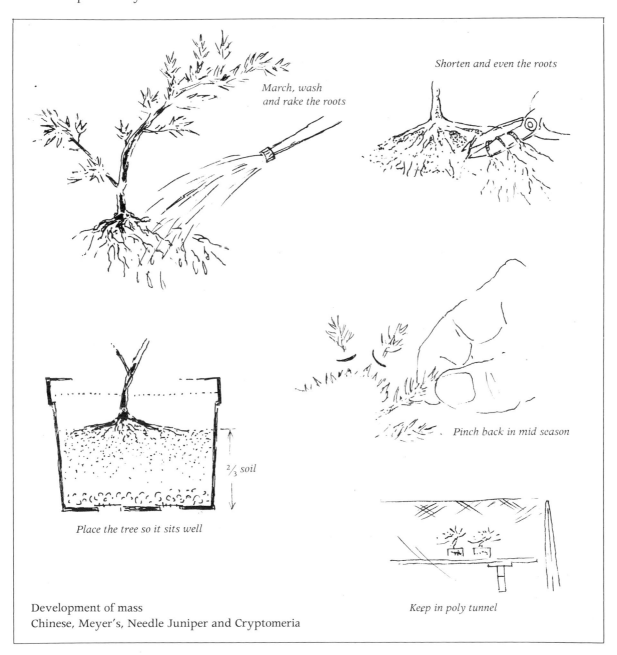

*March, wash and rake the roots*

*Shorten and even the roots*

*Pinch back in mid season*

$\frac{2}{3}$ soil

*Place the tree so it sits well*

*Keep in poly tunnel*

Development of mass
Chinese, Meyer's, Needle Juniper and Cryptomeria

51

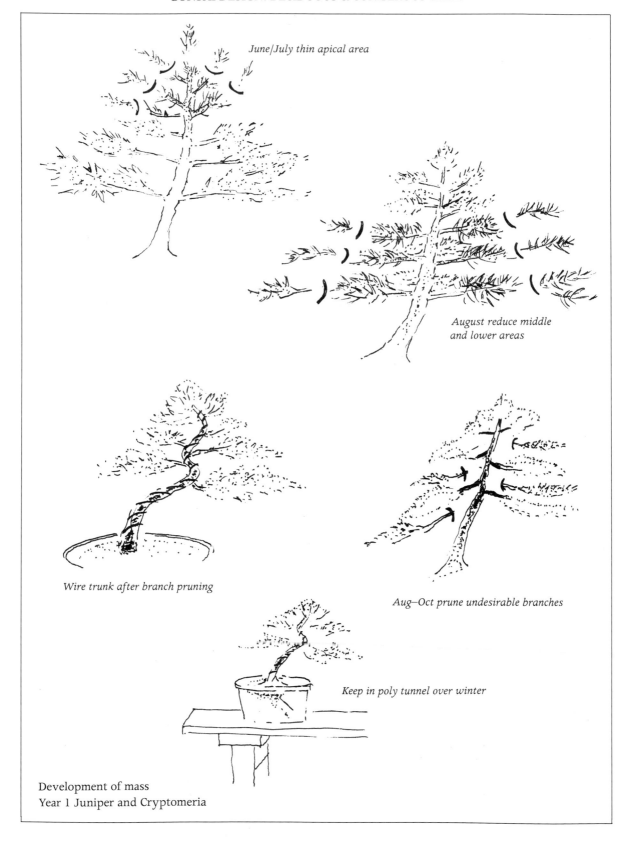

*June/July thin apical area*

*August reduce middle
and lower areas*

*Wire trunk after branch pruning*

*Aug–Oct prune undesirable branches*

*Keep in poly tunnel over winter*

Development of mass
Year 1 Juniper and Cryptomeria

*Transplanting*  Wash the roots and rake them out gently. Make sure there is a good radial placement and shorten the roots till the tree sits well. I use polypropylene pots with a good drainage course and generally fill the pot two-thirds full with soil mix at this initial stage; the tree is then positioned and the soil topped up.

*Placement*  Immediately after potting, place the trees in a poly tunnel and shade lightly. This will act as an artificial humidifier until the roots can translocate actively once more.

*Water*  Water in, using Vitamin B1 solution. Do not be in a hurry to water again until the soil looks and feels dryish. With so much sand in the soil mix the colour will look pale, and a little experimentation will be necessary until you get the knack of assessing on sight the need for water. Never overwater in the month after repotting, as Junipers can develop root rot quite easily. Stick your fingers into the pot to test for dampness. After a month the root tips will be active again and water schedules may be built up to normal. Always mist the leaves with water.

*Feeding*  One month after root pruning, follow the feed schedule for Stage I.

*Pests*  Aphids, red spider and scale are the most likely. Keep an eye open for these and spray as necessary. Cryptomeria sometimes get blight if the humidity levels are too high, so ventilate them well. You need to judge carefully. They appreciate shade and foliage spray but not static air and drenching.

*Shoot pruning*  Using fingers, pinch shoots back in mid season, June and July. Thin and trim the apical zone and upper tree very closely. Allow the shoots in the middle and lower areas to lengthen till August, then reduce by half using scissors. By this means a tapered tree with lively lower branches is produced. The benefits of ventilation and light admitted to the lower areas make them grow fast and also help to build the trunk.

*Wiring*  Wire the trunks in late summer from August through October. Use anodized aluminium training wire. Bend the tree to the projected form and then after wiring, remember to protect the tree from exposure to frost as this can be very harmful. Those trees destined to be styled are wired straight as possible. Delay wiring Cryp-

tomeria until May in Year 2.

*Branch pruning*  Prune and thin undesirable branches before you wire. All heavy upper shoots are removed. All those shoots robbing lower areas of light are removed and in the case of informal trees, those shoots growing from inside the projected bends. Check that the upper tree is not carrying too heavy a load. It is better to thin out than leave a mop. Delay branch pruning Cryptomeria until Year 2.

*Protection*  Protect between November and March in a poly tunnel.

## Year 2

*Placement*  In April, or when the danger of frost is passed in your locale, place the tree on an outside shelf. Cryptomerias will always grow better in the poly tunnel, particularly if much pinching is carried out.

*Water*  Follow the schedule.

*Feeding*  Beginning in March follow the schedule for Stage I.

*Pests*  Spray as necessary.

*Shoot pruning*  In June and August repeat the Year 1 schedule. Cryptomeria will require constant finger pinching to produce a cone.

*Wiring*  Wire Cryptomeria trunks in May and dewire Juniper trunks between August and September.

*Branch pruning*  None on Junipers. Remove any thick branches on Cryptomeria early in the season, around March.

*Protection*  Place in a poly tunnel between November and March.

## Year 3

*Placement*  Trees are removed after frosts and placed on outside shelves.

*Water*  Follow schedule.

*Feeding*  Follow the schedule for Stage I.

*Pests*  Spray as necessary.

*Shoot pruning*  In June repeat the Year 1 schedule. Thin out any dense inner growth. If trunk and

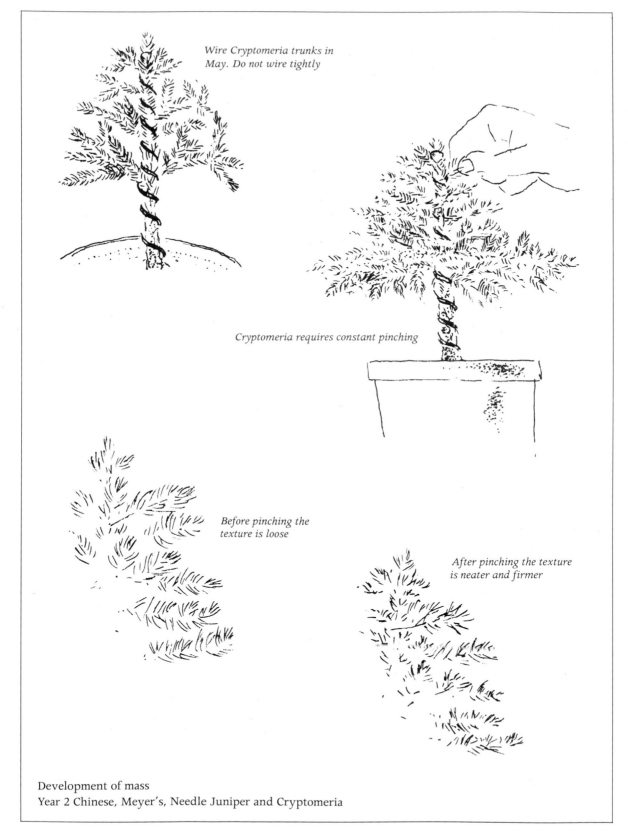

Wire Cryptomeria trunks in
May. Do not wire tightly

Cryptomeria requires constant pinching

Before pinching the
texture is loose

After pinching the texture
is neater and firmer

Development of mass
Year 2 Chinese, Meyer's, Needle Juniper and Cryptomeria

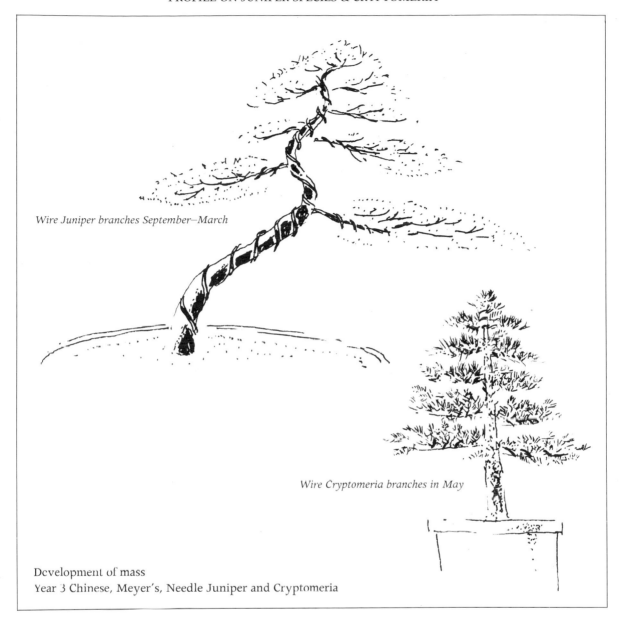

*Wire Juniper branches September–March*

*Wire Cryptomeria branches in May*

Development of mass
Year 3 Chinese, Meyer's, Needle Juniper and Cryptomeria

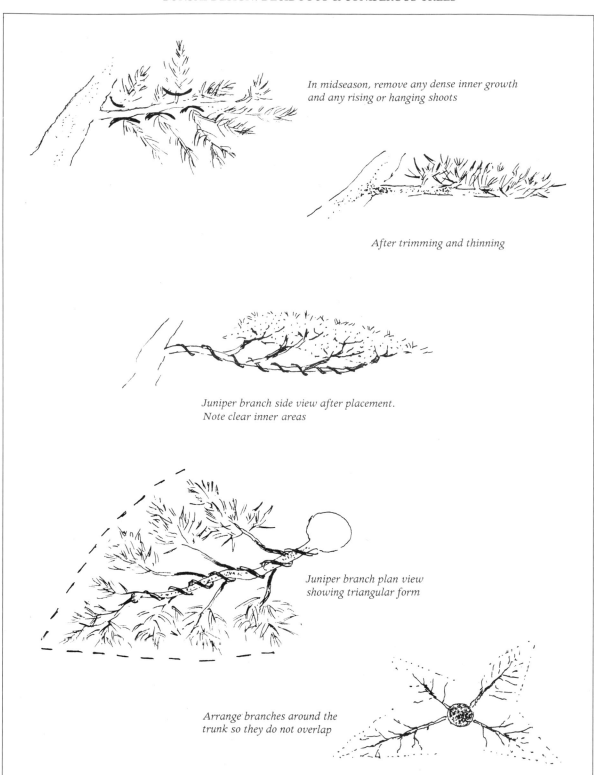

In midseason, remove any dense inner growth
and any rising or hanging shoots

After trimming and thinning

Juniper branch side view after placement.
Note clear inner areas

Juniper branch plan view
showing triangular form

Arrange branches around the
trunk so they do not overlap

Development of mass
Year 3 Chinese, Meyer's, Needle Juniper and Cryptomeria

branch, and twig junctions are kept clear of new sprouts, the emergent branch system will remain healthy. Clean off wild shoots that rise or drop. Keep Cryptomeria in poly tunnel after pinching and pruning.

*Wiring*　Wire Juniper branches between September and March. Dewire Cryptomeria trunks in March and wire their branches in May. Use anodized aluminium wire and coil gently and not too tightly.

*Branch pruning*　Remove only those branches that mar the lines.

*Protection*　Place in the poly tunnel between October and March. It is important to protect wired branches early from frosts and winter winds.

### Year 4

*Placement*　Remove trees from winter quarters after frosts have passed and place outside.

*Water*　Follow the schedule.

*Feeding*　Follow the schedule for Stage I.

*Pests*　Examine regularly and spray if necessary.

*Shoot pruning*　Finger pinch for density. Keep Cryptomeria in poly tunnel after pinching and wiring.

*Wiring*　Dewire Cryptomeria branches in March and Juniper branches in September. Consider detailing the head area of Cryptomeria by trimming and thinning between March and May. Junipers may have their head areas arranged with wire.

*Branch pruning*　No major reductions but thin inner branch growths in August and September.

*Protection*　Move in to poly tunnel over winter.

## Structure and form

### Year 5

*Placement*　Keep in poly tunnel till May.

*Transplanting*　The trees are repotted in March. Root prune lightly after combing out the system. Shorten everything and ensure that the radial root placement is still satisfactory. If downward facing, hooked roots are found, prune them short. Repot in to an 'approximation' container that has roughly the proportions of the desired final pot.

*Water*　After transplanting, water in with Vitamin B1 solution. Water leaves daily. Wait until the

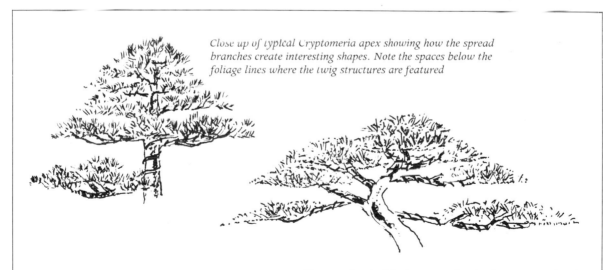

*Close up of typical Cryptomeria apex showing how the spread branches create interesting shapes. Note the spaces below the foliage lines where the twig structures are featured*

*Close up of typical Juniper apex showing how to spread and contour the area. Always thin out as you wire*

Development of mass
Year 4 Chinese Juniper, Meyer's, Needle Juniper and Cryptomeria

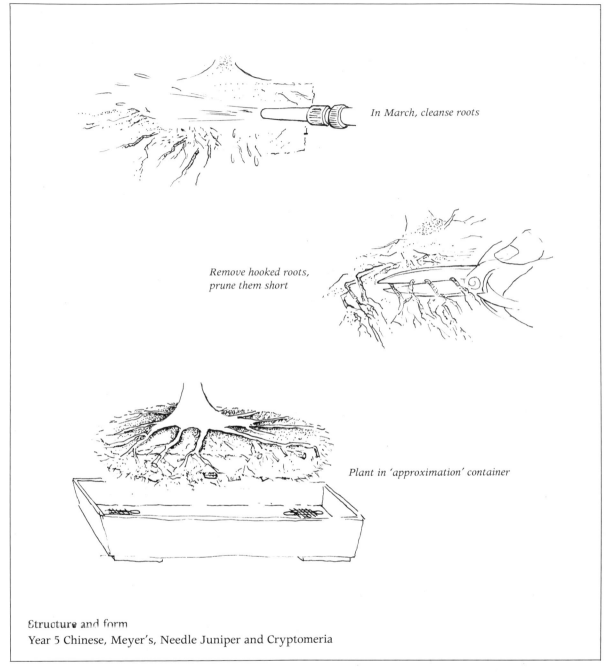

*In March, cleanse roots*

*Remove hooked roots,
prune them short*

*Plant in 'approximation' container*

Structure and form
Year 5 Chinese, Meyer's, Needle Juniper and Cryptomeria

soil looks dryish before watering again. Normal watering schedules are resumed once the budding is strong and the leaf colour good. It is advisable to keep the trees indoors this season so that they may develop fast with the extra humidity.

*Feeding*   No feeding until the end of May, when the schedule for Stage II is followed.

*Pests*   Examine regularly and treat.

*Shoot pruning*   Maintain by light finger pinching. Remove offending dense areas and rising and falling shoots.

*Wiring*   Dewire Junipers. No further wiring at the moment.

*Branch pruning*   Just enough to lighten the mass and create interesting contours and spaces.

*Protection*   Keep in poly tunnel till Year 6.

58

# Refinement of image

## Year 6

*Placement*    Place outside after frosts.

*Water*    Follow schedule.

*Feeding*    Follow schedule for Stage II.

*Shoot pruning*    Shoot pinch in April. By this time foliage pads will be full and buds must be pinched to keep growth compact, and not so lush that lines and modelling are lost.

*Wiring*    Fine detailed branch wiring is carried

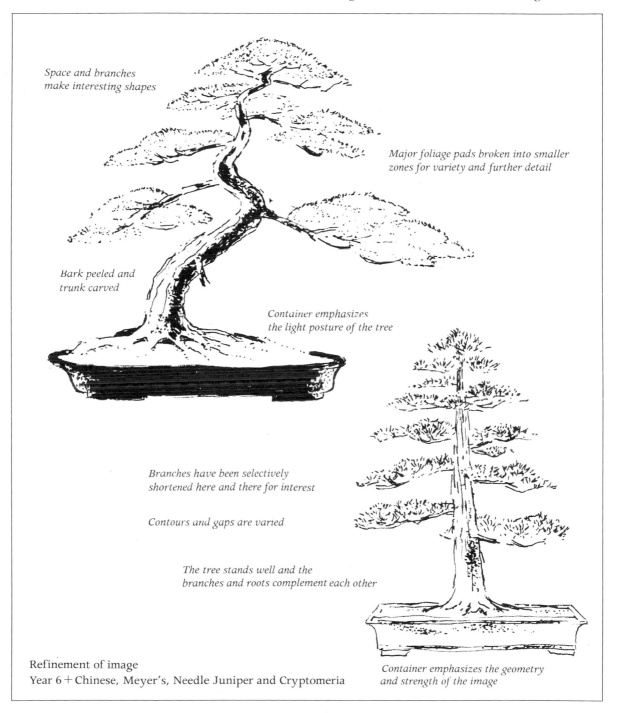

*Space and branches make interesting shapes*

*Major foliage pads broken into smaller zones for variety and further detail*

*Bark peeled and trunk carved*

*Container emphasizes the light posture of the tree*

*Branches have been selectively shortened here and there for interest*

*Contours and gaps are varied*

*The tree stands well and the branches and roots complement each other*

Refinement of image
Year 6 + Chinese, Meyer's, Needle Juniper and Cryptomeria

*Container emphasizes the geometry and strength of the image*

## Table 3:3 Summary chart of the development of Juniper and Cryptomeria Bonsai

| | Stage I<br>Development of mass | | |
|---|---|---|---|
| | YEAR 1 | YEAR 2 | YEAR 3 |
| JAN | | Keep damp ————————————————→ | |
| FEB | | Keep damp ————————————————→ | |
| MAR | Transplant trees into Polyprol pots. Use open soil. Water in with Vit. B1 Solution. Place in poly tunnel. | Remove any heavy growth on Cryptomeria. Keep moist. Follow feed schedule for Stage I. | Follow feed schedule for Stage I. Dewire Cryptomeria trunks. |
| APR | One month after transplanting follow the feed schedule for Stage I. Spray for pests. Keep moist. | Place Juniper outside after frosts are past. Cryptomerias are better kept in the poly tunnel. Keep moist. Spray for pests. | As April Yr 2 care. |
| MAY | | Wire trunks of Cryptomeria. | Wire Cryptomeria branches. As April Yr 2 care. |
| JUNE | Finger pinch shoots. Trim apecal areas and upper tree. Follow April care. | Follow June Yr 1 care. Pinch Cryptomeria to keep the growth conical in overall form. | As June Yr 2 |
| JULY | | | Thin any dense growth. Clean out branch junctions. |
| AUG | Wire the trunks of Juniper. Prune branches. Prune shoots in the middle and lower areas of the tree. | Dewire Juniper trunks. Proceed as for August Yr 1. | Keep trees lightly pinched over. Any branches to be removed can be taken now – October. |
| SEPT | Follow April care. Keep damp. | Follow Yr 1. | Keep damp. Juniper branches may be wired now – March. |
| OCT | Keep damp. | | |
| NOV | Keep damp. | ↓ | ↓ |
| DEC | Keep damp. | | |

|  | Stage II<br>Structure and form | Stage III<br>Refinement of image |
|---|---|---|
| YEAR 4 | YEAR 5 | YEAR 6 |
| Follow Feed schedule for Stage I. Dewire Cryptomeria branches. Finish wiring Juniper branches. | Repot trees. Clean roots and place tiles beneath trunk area. Water in with Vit.B1 solution. Keep damp. Mist leaves. Dewire Junipers. | Follow feed schedule for Stage II. |
| Detail head area of Cryptomeria now – May. Juniper's head areas may be arranged with wire. Follow April Yr 2 care. | Keep in poly tunnel. | Place outside after frosts. Pinch foliage early. |
| Allow trees to grow without too much pruning. | End of May follow feed schedule for Stage II. Pinch trees. Follow schedule for Yr 4 care. | Branch lengths may be adjusted for artistic reasons. Open interiors to display the lines. |
| Thin inner growth now – September. | | Some wiring for cosmetic reasons to neaten the forms. |
| Keep damp. | | |

out during the summer and the wires are removed next spring.

*Branch pruning*   It is a good idea to pay attention to branch length: the combination of long and short lends great charm and is easily managed. It is a way of introducing character and avoiding too perfect a pyramidal form. Think also of opening branch interiors to show further twig and lower branch lines.

*Protection*   Protect each winter.

Repot every four years and repeat the schedules of Years 4, 5 and 6, for maintenance.

Junipers and Cryptomeria were easier to obtain thirty years ago than they are now. In the British nurseries, old stock plants and mature, open-ground examples were then freely obtainable.

There was seldom anything nicer than a 'nursery crawl' on a weekend. The staff of these places thought you were mildly certifiable doing obeisance to a trunk often buried in grass or wrapped in sacking. In Holland in those days 'Bonsai' was an unknown word and you had to say, 'Dwerg-Boom' to be vaguely understood; only vaguely! The tendency was for the staff to identify with their British counterparts and to humour my visits as an easy route to offloading otherwise unsaleable plants. The goodies were carried off and lashed to the back of a Vespa scooter for the long haul home, which punctuated as it was by celebratory pauses, often took on an hallucigenic quality where trunks became elastic in calibre, and the foliage, thick clouds of trained leaves, rather than the misbegotten, tatty reality!

I had access to a deeply-dug flower border, pillaged from my long suffering father, and this sandy area soon produced miraculous changes in the colour and density of the foliage. I used to pour gallons of Liquinure over the plants and they loved it.

I began reading avidly when the first books arrived in England and found that my sandy flower border, with its rapid drainage, was indirectly confirmed as the right way to go, by the recommendations of Kan Yashiroda, who in the late fifties was advocating up to nine parts sand to one of leaf mould for general use with coniferous Bonsai. Such smug justification! This basic combination of sand and organic material, backed up with adequate water and feed, I subsequently adopted for most plants. The success of this procedure was again confirmed with the arrival of the first plants in England from the Kanto plain growing area in Japan, where huge quantities of fine river sand combined with minimal amounts of organic material, supported something in the order of *fifty* widely different species!

The roots on these trees had to be seen to be believed! The tissue of the roots was fine, with the minimum of over-heavy cables. The strength of the top growth on all the Junipers and Cryptomerias was obviously supported and vigorously counter-balanced with the wonderfully dense root systems.

The trees always arrived in February and, at that time, winters were cold. I would automatically place all these newly acquired treasures in the poly tunnel to protect them against frost and to redress the desiccation effects of the compulsory fumigation prior to their leaving Japan. There were always some dried up leaf areas to be found where the gas had found tiny gaps in the bark. In general, the Cryptomerias would show some reddish winter colour, discernible from gas damage by its being confined to the upper face of each foliage pad. The extra moisture and humidity in the poly tunnel would reverse the colour inside a month.

Junipers tended to be affected the same way. With Needle Junipers it was fascinating to see where the growth had been scissor pruned in the fall to provoke tight budding in the spring. Late feeding, still evident in spent feed cakes, combined with the trim, produced wonderful, *pink* leaf tips in early spring. The vigour was amazing.

Not all importation damage was caused through gas. There was one great occasion when everything had been deep frozen instead of chilled *en route* and there were freeze-dried trees everywhere. It was tragic!

The Cryptomerias inside the poly tunnel started producing pink root tips all the way up the trunks and I tried rooting trained branches. I first wrapped the desired root zones with sphagnum moss soaked in rooting liquid and placed the trees under intermittent mist: they were fully detachable inside three weeks. The apecal zones yielded exquisite mame-size trees, and the branches, even thicker versions.

I found I could take enormous liberties in the

time span of repotting Chinese Juniper, if the poly tunnel was used afterwards. The right type of humidity seemed to be the key to many aspects of the styling of these species. I remember being given an ailing, Literati-style Juniper with tight, miserable foliage and planting it in 100% aquarium gravel under mist and watching plumose new needle growth develop inside a two-month period. Existing foliage always yellows as the new tips push through blue and green.

I found Meyer's Juniper resented late repotting when the tree was wired heavily. I tried late repotting, even without wire, and discovered the tree still resented it. I found also that tight wiring of fine growth was dangerous, despite mist to correct the tissue drying up. So mid-season potting, i.e between March and April, is the best all round time for this Juniper. The wiring programme seems safer delayed to a time when this tree is settled. When well rooted, fed and watered, it is a positive delight and quickly produces dense growth that enables the grower to achieve speedily an advanced structure inside a modest time scale.

Japanese Hornbeam

# PART TWO. THE CASE HISTORIES

# 4 Stage I: Development of mass

## Stage I: Development of mass

## Tree No. 1  English White Elm Raft Style

### Time Scale Chart    Tree No. 1    English White Elm Raft Style

| Cutting taken in 1983 | 1984 | 1985 | 1986 | 1987 | 1988 | 1989 | 1990 |
|---|---|---|---|---|---|---|---|
| Root establishment | Grown as Informal → | | Styled as raft | | Repotted in spring → | | Next repot |
| Trunk development | Grown as Informal → | | Wired | Dewired | Grown as raft Develop heavy trunk as necessary → | | Next repot diagonal placement |
| Branch training | Fine wiring and shoot pruning → | | | | → | Leaf prune | Leaf prune |
| Root development | Grown without disturbance → | | Half old root taken Half re-modelled to lay flat | Minor repot  Roots all along trunk → | | | Major repot old root removed |

### Root establishment

The Raft began life as a cutting taken from a hedgerow. The mother tree, which grew near my home in Farnham, had succumbed to the Dutch Elm epidemic and I determined to preserve this local plant and to Bonsai and popularize it if at all possible. The white variegated leaf form is reasonably unusual and the corky bark, fine twigs and leaves that readily reduce with trimming, all combine to make it a handsome tree for Bonsai.

I took the cutting in 1983 and grew the plant for two years as an Informal Upright with the typically curving trunk and branch system of the style. It occurred to me that it could make a fine Raft in the future rather than another run-of-the-mill Upright, so in the spring of 1985 I followed the usual Raft conversion technique of cutting bark windows on the side to be lowest, washed the root system and cut away enough roots of the potential lower face to permit the trunk to lie down. I also wired all the branches and cut away all those which were on the future lower face.

A plastic seed tray was used as a temporary container and tie wires were first passed up through the drainage holes to secure the trunk in position. The initial soil mixture was sandy to ensure a good ramification of roots. The tree was laid down and the wires tied to locate the angle and to immobilize the plant so that new emerging roots would not be damaged with sudden movement. I topped the soil up so two-thirds of the recumbent trunk was covered and mounded the soil over the upper side of the root system. Some intractible upper roots were removed to lower the line. The tree was then styled by lifting and bending the pre-wired branch/'trunks' into position, was watered and then placed inside a poly tunnel.

### Trunk development

The base trunk soon began throwing further shoots, some of which were selected, and all others were rubbed off. The new 'trunks' became tree-like once they had settled and been dewired in the spring of 1987. They produced side shoots which added the feeling of layering to the planting.

I envisage using a larger, longer pot in the

**English White Elm (Raft Style) 13 trunks**
Height 35.5 cm (14 in), spread 58.5 cm (27 in).
6 years from a cutting.
Dark brown unglazed oval,
45 cm (18 in) × 30 cm/12 × 3.5 cm ($1\frac{1}{2}$ in)
(Photograph taken September 1989.)

future and perhaps in the process, developing a couple of heavier, taller trunks to give additional perspective through the use of thicks and thins. A change of major axial placement so that the whole arrangement is more diagonal will also enhance the perspective, as the tall and heavy give way to the smaller trunks.

## Branch training

To date most branch training has been accomplished by fine wiring and shoot pruning. In 1989 I leaf pruned the plant and reduced the size. This increased 'twigginess' without too much scissor pruning into old wood, which can spoil the taper. I foresee the branch system as being typically Elm-like: upswept with a gnarled character and borne in distinct fanlike forms, almost like giant broccoli.

## Root development

The new roots have become so strong along the recumbent trunk and the base of the new branches that in 1990, when I next repot, I shall remove nearly all the original root mass, preserving only those roots which for aesthetic reasons must be kept.

## Future evolution

I see this design evolving towards a stage where there are distinct groups of trunks of differing heights and weights within the mass. The form could remain tall and gentle, or perhaps be lower, powerful and windswept like the deciduous trees on a headland near the sea. The planting would look well in a flat container of great length to imply space, or on a slab where again the mood could change to something more dynamic.

English White Elm –
future evolution

# Stage I: Development of mass

# Tree No. 2  Chinese Elm Informal Upright Style

## Time Scale Chart    Tree No. 2    Chinese Elm Informal Upright

| Taken as a cutting in 1982 | 1983 | 1984 | 1985 | 1986 | 1987 | 1988 | 1989 |
|---|---|---|---|---|---|---|---|
| Root establishment | Roots developed in half tray | | Repotted in spring | Potted in Bonsai pot | Undisturbed | | → |
| Trunk development | Wired in August. Trunk shortened | 2 shoots chosen. Free growth until August then reduced by 50%. Wired Trunk de-wired. | Repeat 1983 & 1984 care | | | | → |
| Branch Training | Branches thinned Main branches wired | Dewired | Repeat 1983 & 1984 care | | | | → |
| Root development | Roots developed as thick radials in half tray | | Thinned out | Lightly thinned | Undisturbed | | → |

### Root establishment

The tree was started as a cutting in 1982 and I kept it because it displayed good roots right from the start. The swelling at the buttress was initiated at this stage and the rapidly developing root flare can be seen in the picture. I ran the plant in a plastic tray for three years and repotted it in 1985. The idea is to cramp the root a little to make a heavy formation. The roots thicken and web when they are constricted, but do not overdo this! Three years without repotting is the outside limit in a small tray because roots that develop unchecked will often thicken far too much.

When repotting such a root system, wash it and remove the outer roots entirely as these will have generated geometric straights and angles from their development in the tray. Comb out the fine beard so that it flows radially and remove about half. Any lower roots that have become too heavy are also cut off.

I planted the tree in a Bonsai pot in 1986 and the shallow, webbed system of roots formed an ideal

pad. As you can see from the picture, I covered all but the main surface roots in order to ensure even thickening.

### Trunk development

The trunk was shortened to half the present height in August 1983 and the trunk was wire-curved. The shortening strengthened the lower branches and helped taper in the trunk. I selected a pair of shoots in the following spring of 1984 and let them go until August when I reduced them by half, wired them as trunk and side branch and dewired the lower trunk. I repeated this process each season until 1988.

*Opposite:*

**Chinese Elm Informal Upright Style**
Height 25 cm (10 in) × 1.875 cm (³⁄₄ in) trunk.
6 years from a cutting.
Dark brown unglazed oval, 25 cm(10 in) × 20 cm (8 in) × 2.5 cm (1 in).
(Photograph taken March 1988.)

### Branch training

The branches were thinned out each year and any buds that had sprouted between chosen lines were removed. By this means all the branches remained simple and light. It is fatal to retain too much weight if the sense of scale is to be preserved on such a small tree.

The main branch lines were wired to give downsweep and to achieve radial placement. I made the finer shaping in early winter using scissors. This late trimming scars the tree less and allows the grower to see clearly which branches to remove and so on.

### Root development

Being well spread and very shallow, the roots will go on fattening to a point where they will coalesce. It may be relevant at this point to prune a couple of roots near the trunk line and wire them up to sprout as new companion trunks.

### Future evolution

Perhaps it would be pleasing to have additional trunks either close to or distant from the main trunk to give the feeling of a Raft or Root Connected style. Both variations are typical of Elms. The additional trunks would dictate some reorganization of the branches on the parent trunk but this will be worthwhile when the lines work together.

Chinese Elm

# Stage I: Development of mass

# Tree No. 3  Chinese Juniper Group on fibreglass rock

### The idea

The idea is to reproduce an actual landscape seen in this instance at high altitude in California, where a frozen lake covered with snow sported a rocky escarpment. This appeared as a dark profile against the snowy plateau with a grove of small firs.

### The rock

Photograph 1 shows the completed rock. I have illustrated the manufacturing process in another

book, the revised edition of *The Art of Bonsai* published by Ward Lock in 1990, so I will just briefly describe it.

Shape chicken netting to the chosen profile and plan of the projected rock or mountain shape. You will probably need to fold the net in half to provide the base and upper contours. Take time and sculpt the wire till it really shows the form. You can always add additional folded pieces of netting to make further shapes and creases. Wire them on, making sure the edges mesh and are locked

# Time Scale Chart    Tree No. 3    Chinese Juniper Group on fibreglass rock

| | | | |
|---|---|---|---|
| Rock manufacture<br>1. Forming chicken<br>   net rock shape | 1 hour | | |
| 2. Applying fibre<br>   glass mat and resin | 3 sessions about 2 hours each | 6 hours | Allow to cure<br>one week |
| 3. Applying exterior<br>   polyfilla | 5 sessions about $\frac{1}{2}$ hour each | $2\frac{1}{2}$ hours | Allow to harden<br>24 hours |
| 4. Sealer resin<br>   coat | 2 sessions about $\frac{1}{2}$ hour each both top<br>and bottom – bed wire loops into resin | 2 hours | Allow each side<br>to dry 6 hrs<br>between coats |
| 5. Colour coat | 8 Sessions of $\frac{1}{2}$ day each | 4 days | Allow paint to<br>harden between<br>coats |
| 6. Curing/drying time | Allow to harden chemically before<br>applying paint coat so shrinkage cracks<br>are minimal. When painted, allow the<br>whole unit at least 3 weeks drying time<br>in a dry, warm, well-ventilated place | 3 weeks | |
| 7. Planting time | This is really dictated by the<br>complexity of the subject. It is fastest to<br>use pre-shaped material. Have potters<br>clay prepared, plenty of planting soil<br>and ground covers to finish. Fix<br>copious numbers of tie wires to each<br>wire loop. The average planting session<br>may take about 3 hrs | Average 3 hours | |

together. If your rock is going to be long and carry a lot of weight, you should consider reinforcing it with sculptor's armature bar or something similar. If there are gullies and depressions, make sure these will drain away by twisting the planes to provide run-off.

The next step is cladding the form with fibre-glass mat and resin. Use the mat thin to preserve the detail and use several layers to give strength. In this design it was decided to suggest snow by the use of 'rock' that appeared to be composed of white quartz with outcroppings of dark granite. This dictated the type of texture used: the outcrop was textured and built up with exterior polyfilla whilst the snow/quartz area was kept smoother with only a little polyfilla used. When texturing is complete, check the edges, for these must suggest strata. Sandpaper all undue roughness. Remember, exposed rocks will be weather scoured on the windward side, or perhaps glaciated smooth.

Next, seal the whole surface with resin and bed wire loops in to the resin coat to act as plant loca-tions. Allow the rock to cure for at least three weeks. Kill the unwanted shine of the resin with a primascura coat of matt black enamel spray paint. Great fun: a chance to release the graffiti artist in you! Allow the paint film to dry and harden, and then colour the rock with the appropriate stippled blends of enamels, emulsions and exterior paints such as sandtex. Always allow each coat to dry properly, otherwise there will be shrinkage and paint cracking. Allow a further three week drying and curing period, and during this preplanting stage never let the surface get wet as this produces a chemical reaction that will turn the surface a milky colour.

## The plants

Two year cuttings of Chinese Juniper were used. The young plants were trunk wired in March and placed in a shady poly tunnel. They were fed with Osmocote, foliar fed and had water spray regularly to give the foliage a deep blue green colour. They were also pinched regularly for density and to

Completed fibreglass rock measures
120 cm (48 in) × 60 cm (24 in) × 10 cm (4 in).

**Rock planted with 15 Junipers**
Height up to 15 cm (6 in).
(Photographs taken September 1989. The planting of
this rock, with the accompanying slides on the
making of the rock, was the subject of a
demonstration given by Sheila Adams to the Wessex
Bonsai Group in September 1989.)

form little branches of the right size and scale. Two weeks before planting they were branch wired and trimmed. Mosses and lichens were collected to complement the planting. As a final task, tie wires were added to the built-in loops to locate the trees.

## Method of planting

The planting area was determined ahead of time and lined with a spirit marker pen. A ring of potter's clay was added to limit the movement of soil, and the trees were unpotted, shaken largely free of soil, were root pruned and placed on one side. Enough soil was added to the planting area to secure the trees safely and these were then placed in position and tied in with wires. A top dressing of a thin paste of peat and garden soil was added once the trees were planted, and the mosses were pressed into this. After planting, the group was placed to settle on an elevated bench in a shaded poly tunnel.

## Future evolution

Some trees may be shortened and some heavier trunks added to enhance the general perspective. When the horizontal branch lines are more defined, the planting will give a real feeling of time and place.

# Stage I: Development of mass
# Tree No. 4  Meyer's Juniper Formal Style

## Time Scale Chart   Tree No. 4   Meyer's Juniper Formal Upright

|  | 1985 | 1986 | 1987 | 1988 | 1989 |
|---|---|---|---|---|---|
| Root establishment | Lifted in May 2/3 reduction. Potted | ——————————————→ | | Should be repotted | ——————————→ |
| Trunk development | 2/3 reduction from 3 m/9 ft to 1 m/3 ft in May | In October the trunk was hollowed and apex tapered and spiralled | In August the spiralling was hollowed to make a shell | ——————————→ | Finer detail was added with dentist's drill |
| Branch training | Branches pruned back and selectively pruned to channel energy | Branches compact and bushy, good structuring possible in October | Branches thinned and refined in August. Good planes developed | ——————————————→ | |
| Root development | Excellent fibre. All roots vigorous. About 60% reduction to fit pot | Solid in one year! | ——————————→ | Should be repotted | ——————————→ |
| Future evolution | | | | Change to good quality pot | Work branches into heavy, contoured, compact zones |

76

**Meyer's Juniper Formal Style**
Height 90 cm (36 in). Trunk about 7.5 cm (3 in) with a
large root flare. 15 years. Temporary training
rectangle pot.

Prior to major styling 1986.

Close-up of the apex
after carving in 1986.
(Photographs taken October 1986.)

*Opposite:* After styling October 1986.

### Root establishment

The tree was dug from a nursery row in May 1985. The tree had been transplanted regularly but even so had a daunting root mass of almost a metre/yard cubic capacity. I removed the outer third of root mass and soil and root wrapped the tree. On reaching my nursery, I shook off the bulk of the soil and pruned back the roots. With regular transplanting the roots have become densely fibrous and I took the decision to plant the tree directly into a container 45 cm (18 in) long with fair depth. The roots were pruned to suit and the tree was watered in with Vitamin B1 solution after being placed in a shaded poly tunnel.

### Trunk development

With a large piece of material, taper is important and I reduced the tree by removing two-thirds of the trunk to lower the line. I then chose a back branch to use as a new apex and wired this roughly into position. The former trunk line I broke off high and left for later treatment. After the tree had settled, I fed it heavily and watered above and below for a year and a half before attempting serious restructure. In1986 I hollowed out the lower trunk and spiralled the apex using a 12 in electric chain saw. I refined both areas with a router and allowed the wood to dry.

I further refined the areas in August 1987 as a demonstration piece at a British Bonsai Convention. Using a router I opened the spiralling down the front to form a sculpted shell. The drying out period enabled me to cut clean: wet wood always feathers. The next step is to use a finer cutter such as a dentist's drill to open and detail the grain. This will simulate age and remove any larger aberrations left over from the use of the coarser tools. The area should be painted with lime sulphur when carving is complete, to bleach and preserve the wood.

### Branch training

The branches were pruned back and selectively removed in 1985. The tree was then fed and roughly scissor pruned to keep the growth compact and bushy till October 1986, when I thinned, pruned and wired the tree. The branches were reworked in August 1987 to give greater detail and to smooth and regulate the planes.

Meyer's Juniper

### Root development

The surface roots are already strong and when the tree is transplanted into a broader container, they will be more imposing. I am sure there will be other roots near the surface that can be featured. In the period between May 1985 and October 1986 the tree became rock solid in the pot as the roots responded to the water and feed.

### Future evolution

I see this tree remaining narrowly contoured, with dense sculptured branches in relation to the heavily patterned trunk. Perhaps a dark grey, deep rectangle would best suit the mood of this imposing tree.

# 5  Stage II: Structure and Form

## Stage II: Structure and form

## Tree No. 5  English Hornbeam Slanting Style

With its simple story, I think this tree speaks for itself without a chart.

### Collected tree
The tree was collected in spring 1962 from a woodland site. This plant was actually attached to the roots of a larger tree and although naturally layered, had initially very little root of its own.

### Root establishment
As the tree had so little root of its own, it was necessary to build root fibre. It was established in a very sandy mixture and kept well shaded. The main roots were already formed and it was a question of immobilizing the tree to encourage fine feeding roots to form. By the next season the tree had filled the original small clay pot with solid root and so was potted on. Subsequent repottings were carried out on a regular basis to firm up, and then later, to ventilate the roots that with Hornbeam become extraordinarily dense and must be corrected if the tree is going to prosper.

### Trunk development
Little development has taken place in the last 25 years as the tree has been confined in small pots. The bark, however, has thickened and has become silvery grey.

### Branch training
The initial branch selection has remained throughout the years. A few lower branches have been removed to increase asymmetry. The flat planes, however, were the result of 1963 placement and it is interesting how the branches have remained tapering and lively throughout their life.

### Root development
I feel the pronged root emphasis is visually a little uncomfortable and a flatter, more spreading system would be better. Arguably, selective root removal of the offending surface roots might well expose superior lower ones. Or the tree could be layered and so furnished with a completely fresh ring of roots.

### Future evolution
I like the gentle, British image portrayed here. I feel the tree could have a more interesting branch line and perhaps the odd longer branch may well do it. The tree often suggests to me the feeling of a ship heeling in the wind.

*Note* – The tree was actually sold, repurchased and sold again and is now prospering with its new owner in the Midlands. Artists often buy back their own pictures and as a trained painter, I find it interesting that, like other art forms, Bonsai are becoming increasingly valued among discerning collectors.

English Hornbeam

**English Hornbeam Slanting Style**
Height 45 cm (18 in). Trunk 5 cm (2 in).
Approximately 45 years, from a collected tree.
Grey brown glazed rectangle,
25 cm (10 in) × 20 cm (8 in) × 6.25 cm (2½ in).
(Photograph taken 1986.)

82

# Stage II: Structure and form

# Tree No. 6  Chinese Elm Group Style

### Root establishment

All the trees were raised by cuttings in 1974. The cuttings were raised under mist and produced good solid roots in about three weeks. At that time I was greatly involved with propagation and raised several hundred cuttings each year. This clone of Chinese Elm came originally from Seitaro Arai in Yokohama and is the variety called 'Suberosa' or Cork Bark.

The cuttings were weaned off the mist and transplanted to larger trays for a year of root development and feeding in the poly tunnel. In spring 1975 they were bedded outside in a mix of peat, pine needle and spent mushroom compost. The beds were raised and laid on black polythene to prevent the formation of tap roots. As the season progressed the cuttings were fed with Osmocote and several other feeds and were kept carefully watered. Growth was amazing! I used to be kept busy keeping top growth in check and soon took to gathering all the shoots upwards in my hand and chopping straight through, a method I suggested in the formation of Broom trees. As soon as the shoots were released, the rough trim periphery looked quite tree-like.

I maintained this system for three seasons and then cut the trees out in March 1978 to make this group. The trees were selected by height and weight and were literally cut out of the deep growing beds with scissors. All heavy lower roots and cable-like surface roots were removed and care was taken to smooth the cut ends with sharp scissors. Unless you have grown Chinese Elm in bulk, that statement will be lost: it means the roots are spongy and call for sharp blades so that they are cut clean and not crushed. It is easy to overlook this point and so unknowingly introduce root problems.

The trees were assembled using nuclear placement and the root pads were cut to accommodate the desired adjacencies. The roots were so dense and fibrous that this sectioning operation was as easy as it was safe. The lower surfaces were evened and angled so that the trees stood well.

As I prepared the container, I passed several wires up through the drainage holes to locate the trees securely. Drainage course and main soil were added and then the trees were test placed. This group was one of maybe 15 to 20 that I assembled one weekend, and with each I tried to keep the arrangement compact and to allow plenty of root run inside the new container. Once happy with the arrangement, the trees were wired in and soil was added to make up the level. The group was later shaded inside a poly tunnel.

### Branch training

The branches were chaotic! Although the beehive trimming is fast and gives a quick Broom effect, it also gives a dumb-bell appearance if used too often in the growing season, as the pollarded branch tips swell heavily. I removed, I suppose, about 50% of all branches, also taking obvious design nasties like inpointing limbs, dropped branches, overdense limbs, knots of limbs and sub-branches and twigs. I cut long, leaving stubs, remembering I had to cut close at the *end* of the season to avoid football-like callusus reforming.

The framework was quite pleasing once it was lightened and soon responded to regular trimming with the production of fine twigs. The more detailed removal in late autumn of neglected dead twigs and other remainders of mass production, like offending spurs, calluses from branch removal and so on, helped clean up the plants and give softer lines. I wired the group for the first time in summer 1989.

### Trunk development and future evolution

I feel the ratio of thicks and thins is satisfactory but could be made more interesting by the introduction of a mega trunk in the foreground and a few tiny trunks at the rear. Each year now the group takes on a more settled look but I feel it needs the emphasis of a definite accent and far more space. I envisage an oval perhaps twice as

# Time Scale Chart  Tree No. 6  Chinese Elm: Group Style

| Cuttings taken in 1974 | 1975 | 1976 | 1977 | 1978 | 1979 | 1980 | 1981 |
|---|---|---|---|---|---|---|---|
| Root establishment | Cuttings bedded out ————————→ | | | Cuttings selected and cut from beds. All heavy roots removed. Group assembled ————————→ | | | Repotted |
| Branch training | Trees rough shaped as beehives ————————→ | | | Branches reduced by 50%. Thinned of faulty twigs etc. Cleaned up in autumn ————————————————————————————→ | | | |
| Trunk development | Thicks and thins and different heights assembled ———————————————————— Ratio kept constant by selective | | | | | | |
| Future evolution | In 1990 onwards, more trunks will be added and a bigger pot will be used | | | | | | |

| 1982 | 1983 | 1984 | 1985 | 1986 | 1987 | 1988 | 1989 |
|------|------|------|------|------|------|------|------|
| | | Repotted | | | Repotted | | |
| | | | | | | | Wired to simplify |
| thinning of foliage | | | | | | | |
| | | | | | | | |

**Chinese Elm Group Style (7 trunks)**
Height 45 cm (18 in) × 90 cm (36 in) spread.
Dark brown unglazed oval,
60 cm (24 in) × 47 cm (15¾ in) × 6.25 cm (2½ in).
(Photograph taken September 1989.)

Chinese Elm –
future evolution

long, and this combined with the taller, heavy tree and outliers of tiny dimensions would, I feel, have enormous appeal.

*Note* my many students, both amateur and professional, have successfully capitalized on the raised-bed system of growing Bonsai which I and my brother-in-law pioneered in 1971. It is interesting how the many variations on our original theme all seem very successful.

# Stage II: Structure and form

# Tree No. 7  Zelkova Serrata Formal Style

### Root establishment
I imported this tree from Japan in 1983. The roots were compact and fibrous and, as can be seen from the close-up, a powerful surface nucleus was already forming. As I potted the tree I did a little digging and found that there were further roots of good size to the rear of the root mass. The familiar soil composition favoured by my regular supplier of specimen Bonsai trees – 70% river sand plus 30% fine organic material – had produced its usual excellent pad of root which I, and the many people to whom I now supply these trees, so enjoy. Once again I was free to sculpt and rake out the dense fibre thus formed and to turn the tree to gain the best root and trunk line.

### Trunk development
The trunk has been well grown and slowly too, as

## Time Scale Chart   Tree No. 7   Zelkova Serrata Formal Style

| | 1983 | 1984 | 1985 | 1986 | 1987 |
|---|---|---|---|---|---|
| Root establishment | Roots good; further roots exposed at potting up | | Repotted using new pot to get better view of root | | |
| Branch training | Pinched back regularly. All inners growths removed | | New planting angle enhances branches | Leaf pruning, keep lines compact. Slow, lower branch extension | |
| Trunk development | Satisfactory taper | | New angle improves the tapered line | | |
| Future evolution | Lower branches extended over next 10 years to give beautiful, asymmetrical, conical form | | | | |

illustrated by the gradual taper without major cuts. There was a single chop at the top to improve taper but this was done well and the local branches utilized to replace the leader and form a small crown. I decided to turn the tree through 180° to give a more balanced view of the tapered branch and trunk display. Based on bark development of trees I have raised, I guess the age to be about 25 years.

### Branch training

In accord with the trunk development, the branches showed evidence of slow formation with only a few chops which had obviously been made to improve taper or lend character. As always with the *Ulmacea*, there were a few dead twigs; and once cleaned up, buds popped up everywhere and I was kept busy keeping the lines clear and compact. I leaf pruned each year to keep the growth dense.

### Root development

The nucleus is good from the new front as seen from the winter picture, but it is a little *too* emphatic. If the whole surrounding root area was raised so the heavy roots strike across and into, rather than appearing to plummet straight down, the situation would be greatly improved.

### Future evolution

The real reason I bought this tree was to work on the less usual Formal Upright style of Zelkova. I see the form as spreading sideways and making linear branch extension, which is greater than the height of the trunk. This of course will have to be taken slowly to preserve the taper and I imagine it will take another five to ten years. But, what a treasure it will then be! I think the pot is truly in sympathy with the projected form and the colour is nice too.

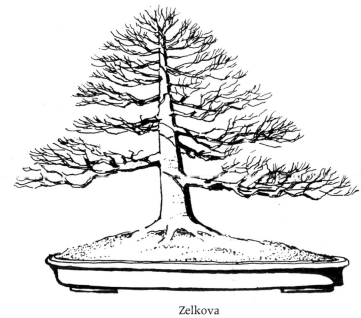

Zelkova

**Zelkova Serrata Formal Style**
Height 55 cm (22 in) × 8 cm (3½ in) trunk.
Grey unglazed oval,
45 cm (18 in) × 30 cm (12 in) × 8 cm (3½ in)

*Right:* Offering picture 1982. Quoted age 70 years.

*Below:* Close up.

Winter 1986.
Blue glazed oval,
56 cm (22 in) × 33 cm (13 in) × 5 cm (2 in)
Made by Gordon Duffett.

# Stage II: Structure and form

# Tree No. 8  Meyer's Juniper Group Style

This is an annotated picture sequence which contains its own form of integral timechart.

The group was put together in May 1989 from material raised from cuttings. The trees range from 20 cm (8 in) to 90 cm (36 in) and were between four and ten years old.

This shows the pot with crocking in position and tie-wires placed.

**Meyer's Juniper Group Style (11 trunks).**
Height 90 cm (36 in) down to 20 cm (8 in)
Light brown glazed oval,
90 cm (36 in) × 53 cm (21 in) × 6 cm (2¼ in).
Custom-made by Bryan Albright.
(Photographs taken during 1989.)

The second picture shows the major and subordinate trees being tried for position. The trees have been regularly transplanted so the roots were compact and vigorous. Two-thirds of the soil was shaken off and the lower roots were then scissored flat to help the trees stand.

Here a small group is shown prior to dismantling for inclusion in the bigger group. The biggest of these was around 60 cm (24 in) tall. I envisaged using these trees with their settled contours to describe the right hand and rear left peripheries of the group.

*Right:*
The major nucleus is in position and the secondary nucleus is being tied. The drainage course and base soil is laid in and the apparently miraculous upright stance of the tall trees is due to tie-wiring the root mass. I branch wired and trimmed each tree as it was placed.

*Below:*
The secondary nucleus has been removed, the better to judge the position of the rear, perspective-making trees.

The elements have been arranged together and final contouring of the soil and branch adjustments are to be made.

*Below:*
The soil contouring is completed and the roots have been combed down into the soil to avoid any suggestion of tangle and confusion. Moss has been placed. It is important not to cover the whole surface and so preserve ventilation and avoid monotony.

The final wiring. Note how the structures flow as compared to the previous shot. The tree has been watered in and will now be placed in a shaded poly tunnel.

*Opposite:*

Four months later. The group was fed with Osmocote in June and the foliage frequently fed with Phostrogen. The foliage was water misted regularly but the soil was kept dryish. This enabled the trees to root readily without drowning in the huge root run the new pot provided; the semi-absorbent body of Bryan's pot also helped. Prior to this picture being taken, I groomed and thinned and carefully wired the branches. The form is maturing rapidly but extra foliage is needed on the secondary nucleus to simplify the lines. At the moment the left hand side works better with its clearer divisions of form and space.

96

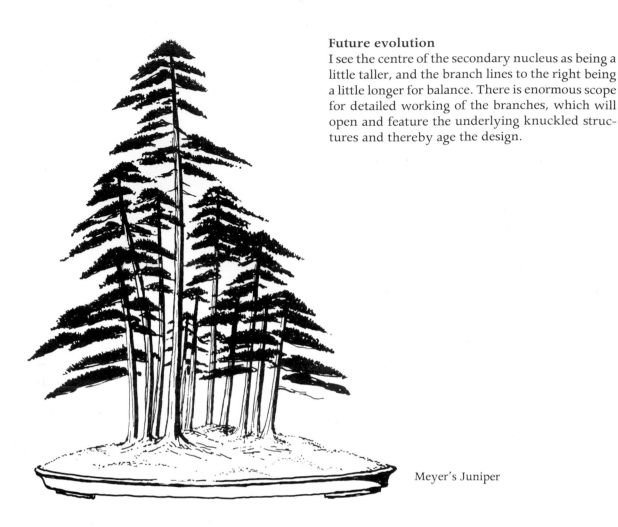

**Future evolution**

I see the centre of the secondary nucleus as being a little taller, and the branch lines to the right being a little longer for balance. There is enormous scope for detailed working of the branches, which will open and feature the underlying knuckled structures and thereby age the design.

Meyer's Juniper

# Stage II: Structure and form

# Tree No. 9  Japanese Cryptomeria Group Style

**Root establishment**

I imported this Group from Japan in 1982. The roots were good and compact; however the top seemed a very dark bronze in colour. The Group was potted into the present container and the new owner happily took it away. However they both returned somewhat *un*happier some months later. Apparently, the bronze foliage had further developed, turning brown in fact. As the roots still appeared fine and the soil still drained well, I concluded the tree had probably reacted to the fumigation on leaving Japan and had become desiccated. I moved it to my poly tunnel and kept it damp.

**Trunk development**

Such a Group is constructed from trees of differing heights and thickness to create perspective. The major tree was 71 cm (28 in) tall and the other two companion trees, around 50 cm (20 in) and 45 cm (18 in) respectively. The smaller trees were arranged in nuclear fashion to constitute conical groups that related within themselves and to the whole.

The problem I now faced was how to replicate these major accent trunks if they were to continue dying back. I chose to feed the Group with Osmocote, to use foliar feed and to spray the foliage with fine water mist each evening. I saved the

**Japanese Cryptomeria Group Style (7 trunks).**
71 cm (28 in) × 60 cm (24 in) spread.
Imported age 40 years.
Unglazed grey brown oval,
45 cm (18 in) × 35.5 cm (14 in) × 6.25 cm (2½ in)
(Photograph taken September 1986.)

# Time Scale Chart   Tree No. 9   Japanese Cryptomeria Group Style

|  | 1982 | 1983 | 1984 | 1985 | 1986 | 1987 |
|---|---|---|---|---|---|---|
| Root establishment | Root mass good on arrival | Trunks replaced with minor root disturbance | Undisturbed | | | Trunk replaced |
| Branch training | 50% of branches lost in Yr 1. By feeding, trees encouraged to shoot out by autumn | All dead material cleaned, branches groomed | Branches stronger, allowed to grow wild to build vigour, then groomed and wired | Structure trimmed to stop infilling, then pinched and wired | | |
| Trunk development | Original balance of thicks and thins was good | Replacement trunks not so varied as originals; foliage match was good | Undisturbed | | | |
| Future evolution | Take apart and reassemble with additional smaller trees to enhance perspective. Use longer and wider container | | | | | |

major trunks, but the minor trunks were lost and had to be replaced using trunks with as close a foliage match as possible. Luckily I had several clones of Cryptomeria raised from cuttings of different imported specimen trees brought over during the last 20 years, and I found a close match. These were replaced in 1983. In the picture you see the Group as still missing another trunk which died and was replaced later.

**Branch training**

It soon became clear that despite my efforts to maintain moisture, the desiccation and die-back was killing off the trained branch frame by at least 50%. By following the feed and mist programme, the trees at last began to fight back and throw out fresh material towards autumn 1982.

In 1983 I cleaned away the dead material and opened the branches to encourage inner bud development. I removed several branches entirely and carefully groomed the branches to clean underlines and to simplify the structure.

In 1984 I just let the trees grow wild and fed and watered for strong development. I then pinched and wired the tree to the form seen and for the

Cryptomeria

next few seasons maintained the structure to avoid infilling.

### Root development
The major trees have good surface roots and it will take a few seasons for the replacement trees to equalize, but this will happen if the trees are kept turgid. The roots expand rapidly when moist and if the existing, satisfactory frame is exposed to the air and the new is kept covered, the rate of desired development is selectively improved and the

young structures can then be given the chance to catch up.

### Future evolution
As the forms become clearly expressed, the trees will become more convincing as separated groups that imply space around and between them as they decrease in size. In aesthetic terms the group could stand being taken apart and reassembled in a larger container, again with additional small trees to increase the feeling of distance.

# Stage II: Structure and form

# Tree No. 10 Meyer's Juniper Literati Style

### Root establishment
The tree was developed from a cutting taken in 1980 and grew in the same batch of plants that supplied the material for the group in tree no. 8. I repotted the whole batch of material every two years, using soil composed of 60% sand, 20% peat and 20% leaf mould. The tree was planted in a 15 cm (6 in) diameter polypropylene pot and developed a solid, dense and very active root pad.

### Training
The trunk and branches were styled together in winter 1987. I was inspired by a famous five-needled pine and wanted to produce a tree somewhat after the image. It occurred to me that Meyer's Juniper, when properly fed and cared for, takes on the stomatic leaf brilliance of the whitest of blue-white five-needled pines — eventually, perhaps, even surpassing them in terms of miniature scale and the daintiness of detail possible, when the small features of this Juniper are carefully used. I decided to employ heavy gauge aluminium wire as this species can be touchy about frost branding in low temperatures where copper training wire is used. Wherever young stock is involved, I avoid the use of copper, despite its extra holding power, because of its all too efficient conducting of temperature. It is also quite possible for heated copper to sunburn sensitive bark and young tissue during a warm summer. If copper *must* be used, shade the tree in summer and keep it frost free in winter.

The trunks were wired first and the bending reduced them in height by at least 30%. By using heavier gauge than strictly speaking is necessary, I have found that the increased leverage will give the same degree of control as a clamp. Allow a substantial surplus length, wire loosely and squeeze the trunk using the hands to grip and spread the load. By using the hands side by side with the trunk totally supported, as if the hands were themselves the clamps, and by gripping tightly, it is possible to bend difficult material.

Once the two trunks worked together, it was possible to wire and place the branches. The original was a Pine and displayed a relaxed twig and leaf arrangement inside the precise geometry of the periphery. I was therefore free to translate the detail according to the nature of the material I used. I employed some extra back branches to give a little foliage weight.

When the tree was finished it sat through 1988 in a poly tunnel. It was treated like the group in tree no. 8, with feeding and leaf spray and enough water to keep it growing strongly and help it recover from all the acute bending.

I repotted in May 1989 when the buds were really pushing. Using the Bonsai container meant losing about two-thirds of the depth of root and soil, although the diameter was much the same. The roots were even and strong and I reduced them, recycled the soil and wire-tied the tree, lightly packing the soil and shaving the root base to achieve the correct angle.

# Time Scale Chart   Tree No. 10   Meyer's Juniper Literati Style

| Cutting taken in 1980 | 1987 | 1988 | 1989 | 1990 | 1991 |
|---|---|---|---|---|---|
| Root establishment | | | Potted in May $\frac{1}{3}$ of root/soil removed. Established in poly tunnel | Undisturbed | |
| Branch Training and trunk development } | Trunks and branches styled together | Tree kept in poly tunnel where it grew strongly | Tree allowed to grow all season. Restyled in September | Remove wires | |

The tree was immediately watered in using Vitamin B1 solution, was placed on blocks to facilitate drainage and ventilation and, after a week or so, to my huge delight began to bud strongly. Prior to the September photograph, I pinched and rewired the tree, but other than that it spent 1989 in a poly tunnel being fed and watered without pruning.

## Future evolution

To replicate an existing tree is a fun exercise that offers a lot of scope in detailed recreation. I have looked closely at the root mass of the original and I think the Juniper needs to be raised by abut 20% to mound the roots. This will also give plant mosses and lichens the chance to age the base.

The branches will need careful adjustment and I can see that relating the branch and twigs and the knuckles below each sweep of foliage is going to be challenging and satisfying.

Gordon Duffet is making a pot that will be closer to the original in feel, although as with the tree, it will be sympathetic rather than a literal statement.

Five needle Pine

*Opposite:*

**Meyer's Juniper Literati Style**

Height 55 cm (22 in), 9 years from cutting.
Unglazed mixed brown round,
20 cm (8 in) × 6.25 cm (2½ in) deep.
(Photograph taken September 1989.)

103

# 6. Stage III: Refinement of image

**Stage III:** Refinement of image

## Tree No. 11  Chinese Elm Broom Style

**Faulty trunk treatment**

In 1990 I would like to attempt to correct the inverse taper. I think it would be possible to repot the tree, and having washed the root mass clean, to split the trunk open and spread the lower portion.

This technique should be quite acceptable to a tree whose family quite naturally produces vigorous root suckers and which adapts itself to British hedge culture, with all the splitting and rough treatment that process entails.

Chinese Elm

I plan to use a fine saw to divide and open the trunk, having first wrapped the surface roots to protect them. A large bladed wood chisel should be enough to split and open the trunk. The trick is to limit the upward journey of the crack by wrapping the trunk with wire above the desired completion point. The roots will be divided and I envisage placing a wedge into the gap to open it enough to flare the base trunk outwards until the outer line is vertical. The tree will be potted and placed in a poly tunnel. The split will be sprayed regularly with fungicide to prevent disease entering. It will be important to use an humidity area to prevent too much tissue drying. I could plaster the wound area with Kiyonal and by carving the trunk at a time of vigorous growth, the super callus mechanism of Elms will work for me and soon bridge the fissure. The alternative is to hollow out and make a feature of the split, as with the Zelkova I hollowed and styled in 1982. Look at the picture of the Zelkova Broom taken in winter 1982. With either method, the trunk has now increased in thickness by at least a third. Some branch rearrangement that will suit better the heavy trunk will now be in order.

*Note* – the further evolution of this particular Zelkova can be followed in an article by the tree's new owner Bill Jordan, in the first edition of 'Bonsai', a magazine launched by Colin Lewis in 1989.

**Chinese Elm Broom Style**

Height 60 cm (24 in) × 8 cm (3¼ in) trunk, 22 years from a cutting.

Photograph 1 (1979). This shows the Elm at 12 years old. The lower branches are being grown on to build the trunk before being reduced to fit the general contour once again. The pot is a 60 cm (24 in) grey oval.

# Time Scale Chart    Tree No. 11    Chinese Elm Broom Style

| Cutting taken in 1967 | 1968 | 1969 | 1970 | 1971 | 1972 | 1973 | 1974 | 1975 | 1976 |
|---|---|---|---|---|---|---|---|---|---|
| Root establishment | Cuttings bedded out | | Transplanted by cutting out of bed. All heavy roots removed | → | | Repeat 1970 | → | Repeat 1970 | → |
| Branch training | Trimmed by gathering up shoots and pruning across → | | Heavy apical shoots removed, leaving stubs. Cleaned off in autumn. Repeat 1968 → | | | Repeat 1968 and 1970 → | | Repeat 1968 and 1970 → | |
| Trunk development | Fast thickening with copious feed and water → | | | Trunk fattening slows after transplanting | Trunk fattening quickens → | | | | |
| Root development | Very fast, giving flare to base → | | All heavy material removed → | | | Repeat 1970 → | | | |

| 1977 | 1978 | 1979 | 1980 | 1981 | 1982 | 1983 | 1984 | | 1989 |
|---|---|---|---|---|---|---|---|---|---|
| Cut out of bed. All heavy roots removed. Planted in ½ tray to control surface roots → | | Repotted into grey oval. Roots flat and dense → | | | Repot into dark grey rectangle → | | Repot into light grey rectangle → | | Repot into blue/green rectangle |
| Branches carefully selected. Surplus removed. Stubs removed in autumn. Lower branch extended | Upper branches carefully trimmed. Lower branches left to thicken trunk | Branches thinned | Routing, trimming. Lower branches thicken | | Lower branches shortened | | Branches carefully trimmed | 5 seasons of slow development | Branches wired for the first time |
| Lower trunk shows substantial buttressing → | | | Trunk thickening below branching → | | | | | | |
| Roots carefully spread to improve surface development | Surface roots rise and thicken as they are con-stricted | Roots look well in new pot | Root buttress echoes the above 'dumb-bell' formed → | | | | | | |

107

*Above:*
Photograph 2 (1983). The tree at 16 years old. More definite tiering has been achieved through pruning and wiring. There is a pronounced bulge appearing below the point where the branches were extended. The pot is a 45 cm (18 in) grey rectangle.

*Opposite:*
Photograph 3 (1984). The tree is now almost 18 years. Despite being repotted and re-angled, the wasp waist between the lower branches and the root mass is worsening.

**Zelkova Serrata Broom Style**
Winter 1982

# Stage III: Refinement of image

## Tree No. 12 Japanese Hornbeam Twin Trunk Style

This tree came originally from Seitaro Arai in Yokohama. It was imported in a batch of assorted deciduous trees in 1976. It was or has been, a hillside tree that had been cut back many times before being dug and turned into a Bonsai. It was a Bonsai in the loosest sense, being a heavy trunk that had three major divisions and a mass of shoots that had been sheared to a domed form. It looked fine in leaf but there was no real weight in any of the branches.

The core of the old trunk was rotted and I decided to remove the central trunk to open and feature the decayed hollows. The carving was the easy bit: with the centre gone, the major and minor trunks looked fine but there were no decent branches. To develop these meant removing 90% of the extraneous twigs to channel energy and so build the chosen points. This took forever! After the first year of desultory top growth, I took the tree out of the pot and washed all the Japanese red clay soil away. I cleansed the roots of any old or damaged areas. There were many heavy roots originating from where the tree had grown in nature. A lot of these had squared off saw cuts where the tree had been lifted and chopped back. Some had rotted and I cut them back to sound wood. The dense roots where thinned by cutting away cake slices between the surface roots.

The difference in performance with the roots in new soil was staggering and the tree budded everywhere. The very thing I was hoping to achieve, however, took many years to accomplish as I did not realize that some Hornbeams take ages to produce thick branches. They are happy to produce miles of twigs but these tend to remain thin. Eventually, by the use of the high nitrogenous feeds and water combination, I managed to spur growth and fatten the branches.

The picture shows the tree reaching a more settled form with, at long last, some appreciable branches beneath the canopy of green.

I have subsequently potted the tree into a much deeper pot and have changed the planting angle to show more of the energy of the massive trunk. When the plant has achieved a larger head, I will restructure and rewire all the branches to produce a more spreading form truly reminiscent of a forest giant.

# Time Scale Chart   Tree No. 12   Japanese Hornbeam Twin Trunk Style

| | 1976 | 1977 | 1978 | 1979 | 1980 | 1981 |
|---|---|---|---|---|---|---|
| Root establishment | Potted in largely original Japanese soil | Soil changed. Old root cleaned. Mass opened | ———————————→ | | | |
| Branch training | 90% twiggy growth removed to channel energy through chosen points | Vigorous growth | | Branches trimmed in autumn | | ———————————→ |
| Trunk development | Central trunk removed to open and feature hollow trunk | ———————————————————→ | | | | Trunks |
| Root development | ——————————→ | | P a d   d e v e l o p s | ———————————————→ | | |
| Future evolution | | | | | | |

| 1982 | 1983 | 1984 | 1985 | 1986 | 1987 | 1988 | 1989 |
|---|---|---|---|---|---|---|---|
| Repot into large training pot | | | | Repot into blue green rectangle | | Repot into deep rectangle | |
| Branches reduced. Autumn branch trim | | | Autumn branch trim | | | Branch growth heavier at last | |
| Thicken | | | | | | | |
| Roots opened between surface roots | | | | | | | |
| | | | | | | | Tree allowed to develop and then restyled |

**Japanese Hornbeam Twin Trunk Style**
Height 71 cm (28 in) × 73.5 cm (29 in) spread ×
15 cm (6 in) trunk. Approximately 60 years.
Blue green glazed rectangle,
45 cm (18 in) × 33 cm (13 in) × 10 cm (4 in).
Made by Gordon Duffett.
(Photograph taken Spring 1987.)

# Stage III: Refinement of image

# Tree No. 13  Japanese Beech Group Style

I imported this Group in 1983. I bought it purely to play with the design which I found reminiscent of the Beech clusters on Salisbury Plain. I wanted to make the periphery rounder and perhaps transfer the planting to a slate or flat rock.

*Opposite:*
The offering picture shows the form of the Group in 1982. The nucleus is simple and pleasing and there is good balance between the thicks and thins.

*Below:*
The close-up shows the pleasing bark quality. There were a lot of conflicting lines and I gradually sorted these out, remembering to leave pruning stubs that could be cleaned off later to avoid large calluses forming. I removed a large section of the main tree to shorten it and improve the proportions of the group.

The winter picture taken in 1987 shows a more integrated form. In spring 1988 I repotted the Group into a larger oval. The branch lines were cleaned and wired and spaces opened in the planting to create a more unified image and to emphasize the different heights within the whole. The Group is maturing but the main tree needs constant management to prevent it dominating. This is simply done by foliage regulation; some of the minor trunks would also be improved with some extra weight.

Japanese Beech –
future evolution

*Opposite:*
**Japanese Beech Group Style (9 trunks).**
Height 83.8 cm (33 in) × 83.8 cm (33 in) spread.
Approximately 50 years.
Glazed oatmeal oval,
60 cm (24 in) × 45 cm (18 in) × 6.25 cm (2½ in)

# Stage III: Refinement of image

# Tree No. 14    Needle Juniper Twin Trunk Driftwood Style

1979 (*Below*)

The tree was imported in 1976 and the first photograph shows it in the spring of 1979. The main strength and attraction of this tree lay in the magnificent driftwood area on both trunks and their relative sizes. Its potential grace was yet to be realized and I concentrated my efforts during the initial period on maintaining even growth of all branches, whilst extending the lines. The tree had too many branches for my taste and I gradually took the offending limbs away, over a period of years rather than stressing the tree by a single operation.

1986 (*Opposite*)

The second photograph taken in late 1986 shows a considerable consolidation and simplification of the form. The driftwood area on the front of the trunk has been extended and the lower left trunk line has been raised. The decision to strip the additional bark was made when it became obvious that the area was in fact dead. I discovered at repotting time that the roots below the right and left hand zones were weaker but there was good activity at the centre front and at the back of the tree.

*Opposite:*
**Needle Juniper Twin Trunk Driftwood Style**
Height 68.5 cm (27 in) × 68.5 cm (27 in) spread × 10 cm (4 in) trunk. Approximately 100 years.

## 1987 (*Opposite*)

The third photograph shows the tree in late 1987 in a deeper pot. The branch growth has consolidated and needs lightening again.

## 1989 (*Above*)

The last picture, taken in spring 1989, shows the mature lines developing and complementing the graceful form of the trunk. In the future I think perhaps the lower left area could be sacrificed and the left trunk restyled as a more dynamic echo on the right.

Needle Juniper —
future evolution

123

# Stage III: Refinement of image

## Tree No. 15  Chinese Juniper Driftwood Style

1971 (*Below*)
This tree was imported in 1971 and the first picture shows the 'offering picture' sent from Japan. On arrival the tree sulked for a year or two and produced loads of needle growth. This was due to the tree being sheared for cosmetic reasons, to look neat for the export picture.

1978 (*Opposite*)
The second picture shows the tree in 1978. The foliage has developed greatly and general health is good. Aesthetically, however, the tree has all the appeal of a pile of green doughnuts and the pot is fairly basic too. The reverse trunk elevation is better than in the first image.

*Opposite:*
**Chinese Juniper Driftwood Style**
Height 83.8 cm (33 in) × 83.8 cm (33 in) spread × 10 cm (4 in) trunk. Approximately 110 years.

**1979 (*Above*)**

The third stage, taken in 1979, is improved. The reverse trunk and branches have been arranged and some lightening of the heavy foliage has been attempted. The new pot is also a decided improvement.

**1986 (*Opposite*)**

This photograph shows the tree some years later in 1986 after a two-man, eight-hour restyling exercise. I grew the branches on for about three years so that when thinned and wired radially and flatter, the extra branch length *at last* gelled with the shape of the trunk. The forms are tree-like and the awful doughnut-like shapes are gone. Great attention was paid to grooming and to straightening foliage planes to emphasize the geometry of the trunk. The lighter pot works better with the new image.

Chinese Juniper

1989 (*Opposite*)
This last picture was a record shot taken in summer 1989. The lower branches have been lightened and the left trunk and branches feel more in keeping with the character of the tree. During the winter of 1989 I rewired and thinned the tree to invigorate it and to further flatten and separate the planes.

# Stage III: Refinement of image

## Tree No. 16  Cryptomeria Japonica Formal Upright Style

1980 (*Opposite*)
The tree was imported in 1980. Most of its appeal lay in the heavy trunk and roots. The branches were well placed but a little neglected, and yellowing of the foliage here and there suggested some sun scorch. I imported the red unglazed oval especially for the tree and repotted it in 1981. The new container was at least three inches longer, but explosive energy of the tree soon threatened to absorb the increase in visual terms. I decided to restyle the tree in May 1982. The idea was to narrow the periphery and to rake the branches down in an attempt to increase the lofty power of the image.

*Below:*
The unkempt tree with vastly over-extended lines.

*Opposite:*
**Cryptomeria Japonica Formal Upright Style**
Height 88.9 cm (35 in) × 66 cm (26 in) spread × 7.5 cm (3 in) trunk. Approximately 50 years.

*Opposite above:*
The lower left branch wired down and groomed. This branch was actually a cheat in that the foliage masks an upward bow in it. The initial upsurge of the branch was very heavy and unbendable without the usual surgery of splitting the fork and bending down. I had decided I wanted a calm looking tree without conspicuous scarring, so I masked the fault with foliage instead of dealing with it.

*Opposite below:*
Typical thinning out and rewiring.

*This page:*
The tree thinned and trimmed apart from the apex.

133

The apex reduced and some wired, downward branch placement.

Close-up of the apex with further refinement.

The sideways shot demonstrates how the tree was developed: note the tapered sloping cut and the branch trained upwards into the leader position.

The final form emerges. Note the sheer visual relief provided when the lower left branch came off. The scale of the whole structure suddenly works.

*Opposite:*

The tree as it appeared in 1986. If you compare this with the offering picture you can see how much the new leader has fattened and become part of a convincing trunk line.

I have now opened the tree to feature the knuckles below the branches and to display the trunk and branch junctions. All lower foliage is carefully groomed away to show the structures to their best advantage.

Something I have not done for years is to grow the species in this book as very small-size trees. Even the Hornbeam and Beech may be encouraged to produce small leaves. Feed is the key and fertilizers that I would recommend for this situation are Fish Emulsion and '0–10–10', both now stocked by Chempak. These gently acting background feeds provide the right support without forcing too much growth.

All these species yield charming results at tiny size. It is worth preparing a micro environment for them as dehydration is the big killer. I used a commercial greenhouse bench tray, filled with grit as a plunge bed, combined with the effects of an humidifier. This worked quite well, especially if the plants were lightly shaded.

Beech and Hornbeam are easily scorched and do well if the soil is mounded and the pot is not too small. Both these species root well as cuttings and this is a good way to raise them as it offers the chance to pre-select the trunk by the choice of the taken piece.

Elm and Zelkova also root easily as cuttings and quickly become twiggy little plants. They too appreciate a reasonable depth of pot and some soil mounding. Root cuttings come into their own at this size of tree and give very characterful results.

Junipers and Cryptomeria develop contorted trunks when cut back repeatedly as cuttings. Remember to wire Cryptomeria straight to maintain formal taper. The bark as it roughens is an added bonus. With careful trimming, the foliage becomes very compact and pleasing scale is created. Not too shallow a pot and remember to mist the foliage daily. Phostrogen is better than '0–10–10' as a feed for this group.

Cryptomeria –
future evolution

## Appendix

Bryan Albright studied painting in the mid 1960s but has always felt happier working with art forms that have a functional aspect. In 1976 he returned to England after a five-year stay in Vancouver, British Columbia where his love of trees developed. He has been studying Bonsai since 1979 and his work in ceramics is self taught. At present he is living in Norfolk, growing Bonsai and also making containers for Bonsai. His great interest is in the integration of a tree with its container as a complete design and he gives talks on this subject.

# INDEX